DISCARDED

Here's all the great
literature in this
grade level of
Celebrate Reading!

Books A–D

Make Way for Sam Houston
JEAN FRITZ

BASEBALL IN APRIL
AND OTHER STORIES

The Star Fisher

The Deciding Factor
Learning What Matters

Seventh Grade
by Gary Soto
✳ALA Notable Children's Book

The Gymnast
by Gary Soto

Woodsong
from the novel by
Gary Paulsen
✳ALA Notable Children's Book

The Land I Lost
from the novel by Huynh
Quang Nhuong
✳William Allen White
Children's Book Award
✳Teachers' Choice

Running Tide
from the autobiography by
Joan Benoit with Sally Baker

**If This Is Love, I'll
Take Spaghetti**
by Ellen Conford
✳South Carolina Young
Adult Award

The Necklace
play based on the story by
Guy de Maupassant

An Owl in the House
from the book by
Alice Calaprice

Cousins
from the novel by
Virginia Hamilton
✳Notable Social Studies
Trade Book

Featured Poet
Gary Soto

yum.

Book A Celebrate Reading!

A Volcano of Cheers

Chasing Your Goals

Maniac Magee
from the novel by
Jerry Spinelli
✳ Newbery Medal
✳ ALA Notable Children's Book

The Talking Earth
from the novel by
Jean Craighead George
✳ Newbery Medal Author

Virtue Goes to Town
by Laurence Yep
✳ ALA Notable Children's Book
✳ Notable Social Studies Trade Book
✳ Boston Globe-Horn Book Award

The Star Fisher
from the novel by
Laurence Yep

Gordon Parks: Focus on America
by Skip Berry

Who Is This Nellie Bly?
from the biography by
Kathy Lynn Emerson

Make Way for Sam Houston
from the biography by
Jean Fritz
✳ ALA Notable Children's Book
✳ Children's Editors' Choice

I Know Why the Caged Bird Sings
from the biography by
Maya Angelou
✳ National Book Award Nominee

They Made Themselves Heard
by Janine Richardson

Featured Poets
Nikki Giovanni
X. J. Kennedy

Book B Celebrate Reading!

The First Magnificent Web

Tales of the Imagination

Nothing to Be Afraid Of
by Jan Mark
✹ Carnegie Medal
✹ Guardian Award for Children's Fiction

The Wish
by Roald Dahl
✹ Boston Globe-Horn Book Award Author

American Weather
by Charles Kuralt

The Weaving Contest: The Story of Arachne and Minerva
retold by Mary Pope Osborne

The Invisible Hunters
retold by Harriet Rohmer

Earthmaker's Tales
from the collection by Gretchen Will Mayo
✹ New Jersey Institute of Technology Award

Sherlock Holmes and the Red-Headed League
play based on the story by Sir Arthur Conan Doyle

Aida
by Leontyne Price
Illustrations by Leo and Diane Dillon
✹ American Book Award

Featured Poets
Jack Prelutsky
Lewis Carroll
Richard Armour
Eve Merriam

JABBERWOCKY

Aida
Leontyne Price
ILLUSTRATED BY
LEO AND DIANE DILLON

Book C Celebrate Reading!

A Better Time Slot

From There to Here

The Princess in the Pigpen
from the novel by
Jane Resh Thomas

The Prince and the Pauper
play based on the story by
Mark Twain

People of the Four Quarters
by Ritva Lehtinen

The Gold of West Africa
by Mary Daniels

Leonardo da Vinci
by Robert Gardner
✳ New York Academy of Sciences Children's Science Book Award Author

Hats to Believe In
by Margaret Cooper

The Wonder-Worker
by Suzanne Jurmain
✳ Notable Social Studies Trade Book

The Witch of Blackbird Pond
from the novel by
Elizabeth George Speare
✳ Newbery Medal

Historical Fiction: An Opportunity and Challenge
by Violet Harris

I, Juan de Pereja
from the biography by
Elizabeth Borton de Treviño
✳ Newbery Medal

A Samurai's Tale
from the novel by
Erik Christian Haugaard
✳ Jane Adams Children's Book Award Author

Featured Poets
William Stafford
Gwendolyn Brooks
Langston Hughes
Charlotte Zolotow

Book D Celebrate Reading!

Trade Books Celebrate Reading!

More Great Books to Read!

The Grizzly
by Annabel and
Edgar Johnson

Where the Lillies Bloom
by Vera and Bill Cleaver

The Master Puppeteer
by Katherine Paterson

The Bread Sister of Sinking Creek
by Robin Moore

Maniac Magee
by Jerry Spinelli

Sweetwater
by Laurence Yep

It's Like This, Cat
by Emily Neville

Let the Hurricane Roar
by Rose Wilder Lane

A Better Time Slot

From There to Here

Titles in This Set

The Deciding Factor
A Volcano of Cheers
The First Magnificent Web
A Better Time Slot

Cover Artist
Pol Turgeon became interested in drawing and collage
while growing up in Montreal. As a professional illustrator
today, he has an unusual talent for putting together
unlike things and creating a beautiful piece of art. When
he has finished a picture, he adds varnish to make it look
wet and "give the illustration soul."

ISBN: 0-673-80076-8

Acknowledgments appear on page 144.

    5678910RRS9998979695

A Better Time Slot

PAR AVION

From There to Here

ScottForesman

A Division of HarperCollinsPublishers

VIA AEREA

CONTENTS

TRADING PLACES

WHAT IS THIS PLACE?   D•9
Time-travel fantasy by Jane Resh Thomas

A WORD FROM THE AUTHOR   D•23
Essay by Jane Resh Thomas

A STORY THAT COULD BE TRUE   D•26
Poem by William Stafford

LUTHER AND BRECK   D•27
Poem by Gwendolyn Brooks

THE PRINCE AND THE PAUPER   D•29
Play by Joellen Bland,
based on the story by Mark Twain

PEOPLE OF THE FOUR QUARTERS   D•53
Expository nonfiction by Ritva Lehtinen

AND NOW FOR SOMETHING NEW

THE GOLD OF WEST AFRICA   D•61
Expository nonfiction by Mary Daniels

LEONARDO DA VINCI   D•65
Expository nonfiction by Robert Gardner

HATS TO BELIEVE IN   D•73
Expository nonfiction by Margaret Cooper

THE WONDER-WORKER   D•81
Expository nonfiction by Suzanne Jurmain

BREAKING AWAY
Genre Study

FIRST GLIMPSE OF AMERICA   D•89
from *The Witch of Blackbird Pond*
Historical fiction by Elizabeth George Speare

A WORD FROM THE AUTHOR   D•103
Essay by Elizabeth George Speare

HISTORICAL FICTION: AN OPPORTUNITY AND
CHALLENGE   D•107
Essay by Violet Harris

I AM SET FREE   D•111
from *I, Juan de Pareja*
Historical fiction by Elizabeth Borton de Treviño

HISTORY   D•124
Poem by Langston Hughes

IN THE MUSEUM   D•125
Poem by Charlotte Zolotow

WHAT A PRECIOUS GIFT, LIFE   D•127
Historical fiction by Erik Christian Haugaard

Student Resources

Books to Enjoy   D•134
Literary Terms   D•136
Glossary   D•138

In the 1500s, bloodletting was a common practice for treating disease.

Messages were relayed by teams of horses.

In 1589 forks were introduced in the French court.

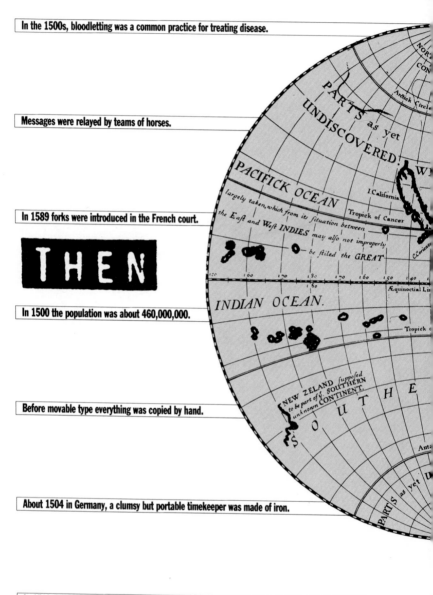

THEN

In 1500 the population was about 460,000,000.

Before movable type everything was copied by hand.

About 1504 in Germany, a clumsy but portable timekeeper was made of iron.

In 1519 the Aztec army traveled on foot, averaging about 1 1/2 mph.

Surgeons use lasers to remove diseased body tissue.

More than 423,000,000 telephones are used to communicate throughout the world.

Plates made of wheat can be eaten as well as eaten on.

The population today is about 5,292,000,000.

NOW

Type is set by computer.

Watches with beepers remind people of appointments.

Cars can average 55mph and more on expressways.

WHAT

Is This

PLACE?

By Jane Resh Thomas

There, Miss Elizabeth," said Sukie, brushing the moist hair back from the child's eyes. "We've sent to the herb woman. She'll bring you something for the fever."

Elizabeth felt herself sink into the featherbed as Sukie pulled the fur coverlet up around her chin. She would soon be warm.

"The fever, the fever," Elizabeth heard the servants whisper, their starched aprons rustling.

Sukie, the nurse, squeezed the water out of a lace-edged handkerchief into the silver basin and bathed Elizabeth's face. The cold water shocked her, but she felt too sick to move away.

"The fever, the fever." She saw Nancy and Martha, new maids-of-all-work from the village, girls not much older than Elizabeth herself, peeking between the blue velvet draperies that hung around her bed. Elizabeth had tried to make friends with them, but Sukie had interfered. The daughter of a duke could not be friends with servants.

"Hush," said an older voice. "Back to work. Her mother mustn't know." That sounded like Mary, the housekeeper, who could sweep everyone but Sukie and Father before her like a broom. The heavy bedroom door clicked shut. It sounded far away.

"I'll undress you in a little while, after you've caught your breath." Sukie tucked the porcelain doll, Mariah, under Elizabeth's arm. She turned the little crank on Elizabeth's music box and, as the song spilled forth, curled the child's fingers around its walnut handle. It played the Summer-music, the air Elizabeth had first heard played from the Queen's river barge last summer on the Thames. The composer Mr. Byrd had created the piece of music especially for the party, a surprise for the Queen.

"I'll be here, my dearie, just outside the curtains, knitting you a warm vest," said Sukie, patting the pocket where she kept her knitting. Her voice sounded cheerful, but Elizabeth saw her cover her mouth with her hands as she turned away.

Elizabeth thought about her mother, deathly pale and bedridden with fever and pain in many joints. "The fever, the fever," she thought.

Puck, the little spaniel dog that never left Elizabeth's side, turned around and around on the foot of the bed and settled himself in the shadows. Then Sukie pulled the heavy blue curtains almost shut. A narrow shaft of sunlight shimmered in the crack between the curtains, fell across the darkened bed, and struck Elizabeth's face. The glare in the gloom stunned her eyes and hurt her pounding head.

THEN

Shakespeare's *The Taming of the Shrew* was first performed in the 1590s.

In the next instant, Elizabeth heard a noise like the screeching of a rusty hinge. Startled and slightly dizzy, she looked around in wonderment, unable to believe her own eyes and ears and nose.

In all her nine years, she had never seen such a wretched place. An instant before, she had been snuggled under the wolfskin coverlet in her bed. Now she stood with pigs surrounding her, jostling her and crowding toward a trough. The sharp odor of pig manure choked her and turned her stomach. Pigs, here in her bedroom, in one of the finest houses in London? Pigs clambering over one another, threatening to knock her down and trample her? But this was surely not her bedroom.

"Sukie-e-e-e," she cried, but the snuffling and grunting and squealing of the pigs swallowed her voice. She clutched the handle of her music box and tucked Mariah tighter under her arm. Lifting her long velvet skirt with her free hand, she turned to gaze around her. Sukie had just now tucked her up in bed, and she couldn't remember going anywhere. What was she doing in a pigsty?

As she turned about, she saw a man standing in a shaft of sunlight that fell across the dusty room and struck Elizabeth's face. The man looked as shocked and bewildered as she felt. He was clearly a peasant, but not one of her father's servants—she knew them all.

Wiping away the tears on her cheeks with her sleeve, she mustered a commanding voice. "Who are you?" she demanded to know. "Take me back to my nurse this instant, or my father will have you hanged!"

At the same time, the man spoke, like the second lower voice in a duet. "Who are you, little girl, a prin-

A production of Shakespeare's *Shrew* has an American Wild West setting.

N O W

cess? And what in blue blazes are you doing in there with my hogs?"

Elizabeth's head was swimming. Somehow she had flown from her own featherbed to this byre, where she struggled to keep her footing in a sea of pigs, Mariah under one arm, the walnut music box still pouring out its sweet song in her hand. It was as if no time had passed.

And this bold peasant was questioning her, a nobleman's daughter, in his strange kind of English. Father would certainly have this man killed. Or at least run out of London.

"You're in some pickle," said the man. As he closed a gate behind him and made his way across the pen, the pigs parted before him like the Red Sea. Elizabeth saw that he was wearing rough blue pantaloons and a waistcoat over a tartan blouse. Scots wore tartan—perhaps he was Scottish. He seemed poorly dressed in a foreign style, but his hair was golden and his smile kind.

A runty pig squealed and stood on its hind legs, imploring Elizabeth like a puppy to pick her up. She looked down at her favorite dress. The gold tracery Sukie had embroidered on the bodice and sleeves glittered in the splinter of sun. But wherever the pigs had brushed against her, they had smeared and stained the claret velvet. 'Tis too late now to worry about soiling my gown, she thought.

"Sukie!" she called again. "Puck!" She had rarely in her life been out of Sukie's sight. As her fear mounted with the approach of the man, she cried out louder, demanding obedience. "Puck! Sukie!" Still no dog, no nurse. Here she stood, alone in a byre with a hundred pigs and a shabby peasant, not knowing how she had come there or where she was.

"Hold it, there. I don't bite, or even growl." The peasant picked her up and carried her out of the pigsty, while the music box played on, a feeble tinkle beneath the oinks and snorts of the pigs.

"Where did you come from, you and these fancy clothes?" The man set her gently on her feet and looked her up and down. "And where are your folks?"

"My father. . . ." said Elizabeth, struggling to calm her queasy stomach and rubbery legs. She took a deep breath and started again. "My father is Michael, Duke of Umberland, advisor to the Queen. Take me home at once!" Waving the music box like a scepter, she almost dropped Mariah in the steaming bucket of feed that stood by the gate.

The man laughed. "And I," he said, one foot on the fence rail and his right hand on his chest, "I'm the King of England."

Elizabeth gasped at the peasant's boldness. "Your head will look down from a pike on London Bridge this day," she said. "What is this place?"

"This? Why this is McCormicks' pig barn, in the state of Iowa. Joe McCormick, king of the pigs, at your service." As he made a little bow, a woman stepped through the open door, with the sun dazzling behind her, making a halo of her hair. "And this here's my queen, Queen Kathy."

"Hello!" said the woman in a friendly way, peering at Elizabeth. "You must be one of Ann's friends. What kind of trick have you girls cooked up? And why aren't you in school?"

As her eyes adapted to the dusky light of the barn, the woman hesitated, looking closely at Elizabeth's velvet gown and the pearls at her throat. She turned to the man. "She looks like she just stepped out of an Elizabethan portrait," she said. "Her costume is a copy of sixteenth-century style." The woman's puzzled voice made a question of the statement.

Elizabeth's head pounded. The music box was running down. "Fetch Sukie, my nurse," she said. "I think I'm going to swoon."

Kathy helped Elizabeth to lie down on a bale of hay and settled Mariah safely in the crook of her arm. Elizabeth saw that Kathy and Joe were dressed alike, in rough blue clothes. A woman in pantaloons! she thought. This peasant queen would be stoned to death for daring to dress like a man.

"She's burning up with fever," said Kathy with one hand on Elizabeth's forehead.

The fever. Elizabeth knew she must escape from this Iowa place before she grew too ill to walk. Which London lane or back alley might be called Iowa? She had never heard of such a street. How far would she have to walk to get back home?

"The fever must be why she talks so wild," said Joe. He put his hands in his hip pockets. "I asked her where she came from, but all she could talk about was queens and dukes and having my head on a pike at London Bridge."

"She's out of her mind, of course," said Kathy. "But where did a kid like her learn about heads on pikes? You have to know something before you can rave about it. And where did she get such a costume?" Elizabeth watched the woman studying her dress. "And look at the gold inlay on that music box. And that exquisite doll."

"What's your name and address?" said Joe, kneeling beside her, as a peasant should before nobility. "We'll call your parents."

Call her parents? Elizabeth had already shouted for Sukie and Puck, but nobody had come. "I am Elizabeth. Daughter to the Duke and Duchess of Umberland, Charington House." She held up the coat of arms carved on the back of her music box and watched them closely. She had heard of kidnappers who held noblemen's children for ransom. She mustn't let them see she was afraid.

"No dukes and duchesses in these parts, Elizabeth. Stick out your tongue." Joe pointed a silver wand at her face, and Elizabeth squinted in its light. "Let me shine this flashlight down your gullet. Does your throat hurt?"

THEN

In 1592, the plague killed 15,000 people in London, England.

"Past saying. And my head pounds." She clutched Mariah and watched the couple's every move, even though the light that burned in the globes on the ceiling hurt her eyes. "The ague has taken me, just as it did my mother. We must have breathed a draught of night air."

"We'll take you to Doctor Davis, our friend in town," said Kathy, brushing the damp hair away from Elizabeth's eyes. She turned to Joe. "I guess we'd better call Sheriff Cox too. We'll find your parents, Elizabeth, but until we do, we'll look after you. We have a daughter about your age. Ann."

Elizabeth thought of the parade of doctors who had treated Mother's fever. Sukie had let her sit in a corner near the bed, where nobody noticed her. Elizabeth remembered what had happened as if it had been a dream. The first doctor had been a man dressed in black carrying prayer books in one hand and a basket of leeches in the other. The horrible creatures had

attached themselves to Mother's skin and sucked—
Oh! It was too disgusting to think about.

Another doctor also wore black, with a white collar turned up. He brought a kit of sharp little knives to open a vein in Mother's arm. The blood flowed into a silver basin. This bloodletting would cure the congestion that caused the sickness, the doctor had assured Father. Mother's maid Dinah emptied cups of red blood, shaking her head and pursing her lips and glowering at the physician behind his back.

When these cures had not stopped the fever, Father begged the assistance of the greatest physician in the realm, the Queen's own doctor. He came to the door in the Queen's gold carriage, wearing a black velvet doublet and gold buckles on his shoes and pearl buttons in a line down the front of his waistcoat. His several footmen came behind, carrying books and rosewood cases of equipment. This physician acted like a king, Elizabeth thought.

In 1990, a new treatment proves effective for chicken pox.

N O W

He clapped his hands, and the footman handed him a vial of rusty powder. This he mixed with wine, which a footman poured down Mother's throat. Then he drove away again in the Queen's gold carriage, with his footmen following.

Oh, Elizabeth remembered it all. Mother had been deathly ill for three days. Dinah had refused to leave her side, but slept, when she slept at all, on the floor beside the bed. She moistened a handkerchief with the broth the cook had made, and squeezed droplets into Mother's mouth.

When she had recovered enough to speak, the Queen's physician returned with another dose of the rusty powder. Mother clamped her jaws shut.

"Her wits are wandering," said the doctor. "Force the potion 'twixt her lips."

Elizabeth saw Mother spit the medicine back in the footman's face. "My wits," she said, as the footman wiped his eyes, "are here at home. I should rather die of the fever than die of the cure."

Soon Elizabeth heard Father shouting in the hall. The physician shouted back, but he went away, and he did not return. Whispering servants gossiped that now, without her medicine, the Duchess would surely die.

A voice roused Elizabeth from her dreaming memories of home.

"Sorry to wake you, Elizabeth, dear." The woman wrapping her in a blanket was not Sukie, Elizabeth saw with alarm, but Kathy. Once again, she smelled the acrid stench of the pigs and saw the globes of light above her head. She could still hear the animals moving restlessly about.

"We'll have to ditch your pretty slippers," said Kathy. "They'll never recover from the pigpen, I'm afraid. No matter how hard we scrub, they'll still smell bad. But your doll is safe in your arms. And this." Kathy cranked the music box and put it under the blanket into Elizabeth's hand.

"I've already started the car while you were dozing," said Joe. "We'll wait there; Kathy's calling ahead to the doctor and the sheriff." As he carried Elizabeth out of the pighouse, she saw the runty pig's blunt face thrust between the fence rails as it watched her go.

Elizabeth's fear melted into astonishment. The tree-lined avenues and the green lawns and the noblest houses of London were gone. She had somehow been kidnapped and spirited away to the country.

And what a country! As far as she could see on every side were perfectly flat fields planted in rows of high, pale yellow plants. The fever must have hurt her

eyes, for in the distance she thought she saw carriages moving in the fields, drawing enormous wagons heaped with gold. But though she strained her eyes, she saw no animals. The carriages moved as if by magic. She held Mariah close, and listened to the muffled music under the blanket.

"What is the gold in the wagons?" she said.

"Corn," said Joe.

"Where are the oxen?" she asked. "How do the carriages go, with no beasts to pull them and no men to push?"

"Oh, you're pulling my leg, Elizabeth," said Joe. "Or are you a city girl? We've used tractors all my life."

First *flashlight*. Now *tractor*. What were these strange words? And these people spoke English with a foreign accent. Were they Spaniards perhaps? Would the Queen's enemies carry off a little girl?

"The car's around here," said Joe.

Elizabeth looked back at the red byre and ahead at a white cottage. In the dooryard stood another coach, long and low, shiny red, and as beautiful as any carriage the Queen had ever ridden in. One end belched smoke. Across the front, an English word was written. F-O-R-D. Ford. But where were the horses?

Joe opened a door in the side of the coach and laid Elizabeth down on the soft plush cushions. She heard a rumble and felt vibrations. The air was warm inside; might the smoke have issued from the carriage itself? She had never heard of a carriage with a hearth.

Joe sat in the front compartment, and soon Kathy climbed in too. She turned and smiled. "We'll be there soon," she said. "It isn't far."

This woman spoke an English so strange that Elizabeth could scarcely understand her. Just then, the carriage lurched and began to move, even though the ground was level, even though no horses pulled and no servants pushed. Yet Kathy's smile didn't fade; her calm gray eyes never flickered.

Elizabeth sat up. Smoke billowed behind as the carriage gathered speed. They raced faster and faster, faster than any horse could ever go. Elizabeth's heart kept pace, and fear rose in her throat.

My wits are wandering, indeed, she thought. The fever has made me mad. She looked out through the crystal casements. The fields and the roadside trees rushed by at an unimaginable speed, yet Kathy and Joe sat calmly watching the road ahead.

Elizabeth felt dizzy. A duke's daughter mustn't cry, but her eyes filled with tears. A duke's daughter mustn't let them *see* her cry. She lay down on the plush cushions, Mariah's cool porcelain face against her own hot cheek. She turned the crank on the little walnut box, shut her eyes, and held the Summermusic to her ear.

As the music played, Elizabeth imagined the green banks of the Thames on the day of the great party where she had first heard that music. The crowd of splendid ladies and noble gentlemen had played shuttlecock and bowls while the quartet sent its song from a barge anchored on the water.

Elizabeth imagined that she heard the rustle of servants' starched aprons and saw Sukie's smile and her round pink face. But now, she realized, she was speeding with strangers in a magical coach toward an unknown town, sick in body and sick at heart. How would she ever find her way home from such a place as Iowa?

Creativity Exercises and the Princess

Jane Resh Thomas

Some novelists begin writing only after they gather notebooks full of research. In contrast, my intuitive methods look like disorganization and lack of discipline, but they work for me.

The idea for *The Princess in the Pigpen** came to me in the bathtub, where I was doing creativity exercises. Imagine yourself in a landscape, my book about creativity had directed me.

I found myself looking down into the cone of an extinct volcano, where nothing was alive except a woman dressed in long white robes. She walked toward me across a rocky valley. I kept trying to focus

*"What Is This Place?" is from *The Princess in the Pigpen.*

on the woman, but she neither said nor did a thing.

I hadn't really expected such an exercise to help me, but having nothing better to do, I imagined the same scene again the next day. Although I ignored distractions and concentrated, the woman offered no help.

On the third day my wish came true. Once more, the woman looked at me with a whimsical little smile, saying nothing, but this time, I let in the distraction. It was an image of a beautiful little girl dressed in a claret velvet dress with a lace ruff at the neck and decorated with pearls and gold thread. She was standing in my Iowa friends' pig-

BY JANE RESH THOMAS

pen with a doll under one arm and a carved music box in her hand. Then the woman I had imagined handed me a tiny white flower, and the valley turned green and burst into bloom.

Now there was work to be done. Who was this girl, and what in the world was she doing in modern Iowa? I wrote *The Princess in the Pigpen* to find out the answers to those questions. It turned out that they had everything to do with my own childhood. My favorite tale then was about an unrecognized princess. I always felt that nobody knew I was royal too.

Whether I am writing stories or book reviews for the newspaper, my purpose is not to report what I already know, but to find out what I think and feel. This way of working is dangerous; I am always finding out things about myself that I didn't necessarily want to know. My stories begin with only the sketchiest kind of outline. Even in junior high, I al-ways had to write my papers first and then write the required outline.

I thought that I knew enough about Elizabethan England to write the novel without research. I was wrong. In the first draft, I made Elizabeth remember hearing Handel's *Water Music* played in 1600 from the Queen's barge on the River Thames . . . but Handel wasn't born until 1685.

So I read several books about the English Renaissance and everyday life in Tudor England for background information. To a surprising extent, my research drove the plot, changing it and deepening the story's themes in unexpected ways.

My groping way of working is not very efficient, nor would it suit a writer who prefers the comfort of working from a detailed outline. Like other groups of people, writers are not all alike. They consequently must adapt general principles to their own uses.

THINKING ABOUT IT

1 You are Elizabeth. You are filled with wonder and alarm. Obviously, you can't buy a one-way ticket to go home again. So what are you to do?

2 Some people would say that Elizabeth is pampered and spoiled. Do you agree? What evidence can you find to support a "yes"? a "no"?

3 This story is a time-travel fantasy. Someone goes from one place in time to another. If you were writing a time-travel fantasy, how would you make it happen? Tell about it.

Another Book by Jane Resh Thomas

In *Courage at Indian Deep*, Cass is still lonely and homesick after living for a year at the north shore of Lake Superior. Suddenly, he's faced with the challenge of how to save a group of shipwrecked sailors.

A Story That Could Be True
William Stafford

If you were exchanged in the cradle and
your real mother died
without ever telling the story
then no one knows your name,
and somewhere in the world
your father is lost and needs you
but you are far away.

He can never find
how true you are, how ready.
When the great wind comes
and the robberies of the rain
you stand on the corner shivering.
The people who go by—
you wonder at their calm.

They miss the whisper that runs
any day in your mind,
"Who are you really, wanderer?"—
and the answer you have to give
no matter how dark and cold
the world around you is:
"Maybe I'm a king."

Luther and Breck
Gwendolyn Brooks

In England, there were castles.
Here, there never are.
And anciently were knights so brave,
Off to bold deeds afar,
And coming back to long high halls
So stony, so austere!

These little boys care nothing for
Their wooden walls of HERE.
Much rather mount a noble steed
And speed to save the Queen;
To chop, in dreadful grottoes,
Dragons never seen.

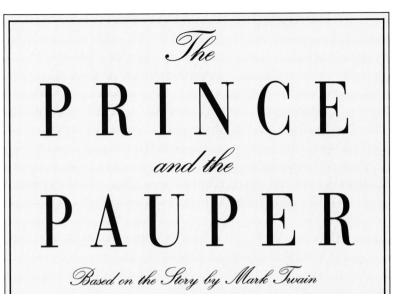

The
PRINCE
and the
PAUPER

Based on the Story by Mark Twain

Play by Joellen Bland

CHARACTERS

EDWARD, PRINCE OF WALES
TOM CANTY, *the Pauper*
LORD HERTFORD
LORD ST. JOHN
KING HENRY VIII
HERALD
MILES HENDON
JOHN CANTY, *Tom's father*
HUGO, *a young thief*
TWO WOMEN

JUSTICE
CONSTABLE
JAILER
SIR HUGH HENDON
TWO PRISONERS
TWO GUARDS
THREE PAGES
LORDS AND LADIES
VILLAGERS

SCENE ONE

Time: *1547.*
Setting: *Westminster Palace, England. Gates leading to courtyard are at right. Slightly to the left, off court-*

*yard and inside gates, interior of palace anteroom is
visible. There is a couch with a rich robe draped on it,
screen at rear, bellcord, mirror, chairs, and a table with
bowl of nuts, and a large golden seal on it. Piece of armor hangs on one wall. Exits are rear and downstage.*
At Rise: TWO GUARDS—*one at right, one at left—
stand in front of gates, and several* VILLAGERS *hover
nearby, straining to see into courtyard where* PRINCE *may
be seen through fence, playing.* TWO WOMEN *enter right.*

1ST WOMAN: I have walked all morning just to have a
glimpse of Westminster Palace.
2ND WOMAN: Maybe if we can get near enough to the
gates, we can have a glimpse of the young prince.
*(*TOM CANTY, *dirty and ragged, comes out of crowd
and steps close to gates.)* I have always dreamed of
seeing a real prince! *(Excited, he presses his nose
against gates.)*
1ST GUARD: Mind your manners, you young beggar!
(Seizes TOM *by collar and sends him sprawling into
crowd.* VILLAGERS *laugh, as* TOM *slowly gets to his
feet.)*
PRINCE *(Rushing to gates):* How dare you treat a poor
subject of the King in such a manner! Open the
gates and let him in! *(As* VILLAGERS *see* PRINCE,
they take off their hats and bow low.)
VILLAGERS *(Shouting together):* Long live the Prince of
Wales! *(*GUARDS *open gates and* TOM *slowly passes
through, as if in a dream.)*
PRINCE *(To* TOM*):* You look tired, and you have been
treated cruelly. I am Edward, Prince of Wales.
What is your name?
TOM *(Looking around in awe):* Tom Canty, Your
Highness.
PRINCE: Come into the palace with me, Tom. *(*PRINCE
leads TOM *into anteroom.* VILLAGERS *panto-
mime conversation, and all but a few exit.)* Where

do you live, Tom?

TOM: In the city, Your Highness, in Offal Court.

PRINCE: Offal Court? That is an odd name. Do you have parents?

TOM: Yes, Your Highness.

PRINCE: How does your father treat you?

TOM: If it please you, Your Highness, when I am not able to beg a penny for our supper, he treats me to beatings.

PRINCE (*Shocked*): What! Beatings? My father is not a calm man, but he does not beat me. (*Looks at* TOM *thoughtfully*) You speak well and have an easy grace. Have you been schooled?

TOM: Very little, Your Highness. A good priest who shares our house in Offal Court has taught me from his books.

PRINCE: Do you have a pleasant life in Offal Court?

TOM: Pleasant enough, Your Highness, save when I am hungry. We have Punch and Judy shows, and sometimes we lads have fights in the street.

PRINCE (*Eagerly*): I should like that. Tell me more.

TOM: In summer, we run races and swim in the river, and we love to wallow in the mud.

PRINCE (*Sighing, wistfully*): If I could wear your clothes and play in the mud just once, with no one to forbid me, I think I could give up the crown!

TOM (*Shaking his head*): And if I could wear your fine clothes just once, Your Highness . . .

PRINCE: Would you like that? Come, then. We shall change places. You can take off your rags and put on my clothes—and I will put on yours. (*He leads* TOM *behind screen, and they return shortly, each wearing the other's clothes.*) Let's look at ourselves in this mirror. (*Leads* TOM *to mirror*)

TOM: Oh, Your Highness, it is not proper for me to wear such clothes.

PRINCE (*Excitedly, as he looks in mirror*): Heavens, do

you not see it? We look like brothers! We have the same features and bearing. If we went about together, dressed alike, there is no one who could say which is the Prince of Wales and which Tom Canty!

TOM (*Drawing back and rubbing his hand*): Your Highness, I am frightened. . . .

PRINCE: Do not worry. (*Seeing* TOM *rub his hand*) Is that a bruise on your hand?

TOM: Yes, but it is a slight thing, Your Highness.

PRINCE (*Angrily*): It was shameful and cruel of that guard to strike you. Do not stir a step until I come back. I command you! (*He picks up golden Seal of England and carefully puts it into piece of armor. He then dashes out to gates.*) Open! Unbar the gates at once! (2ND GUARD *opens gates, and as* PRINCE *runs out, in rags,* 1ST GUARD *seizes him, boxes him on the ear, and knocks him to the ground.*)

1ST GUARD: Take that, you little beggar, for the trouble you have made for me with the Prince. (VILLAGERS *roar with laughter.*)

PRINCE (*Picking himself up, turning on* GUARD *furiously*): I am Prince of Wales! You shall hang for laying your hand on me!

1ST GUARD (*Presenting arms; mockingly*): I salute Your Gracious Highness! (*Then, angrily,* 1ST GUARD *shoves* PRINCE *roughly aside.*) Be off, you mad bag of rags! (PRINCE *is surrounded by* VILLAGERS, *who hustle him off.*)

VILLAGERS (*Ad lib, as they exit, shouting*): Make way for His Royal Highness! Make way for the Prince of Wales! Hail to the Prince! (*Etc.*)

TOM (*Admiring himself in mirror*): If only the boys in Offal Court could see me! They will not believe

THEN
In 1520, King Henry VIII built bowling lanes in Whitehall Palace.

me when I tell them about this. *(Looks around anxiously)* But where is the Prince? *(Looks cautiously into courtyard.* Two Guards *immediately snap to attention and salute. He quickly ducks back into anteroom as* Hertford *and* St. John *enter at rear.)*

Hertford *(Going toward* Tom, *then stopping and bowing low):* My Lord, you look distressed. What is wrong?

Tom *(Trembling):* Oh, I beg of you, be merciful. I am no Prince, but poor Tom Canty of Offal Court. Please let me see the Prince, and he will give my rags back to me and let me go unhurt. *(Kneeling)* Please, be merciful and spare me!

Hertford *(Puzzled and disturbed):* Your Highness, on your knees? To me? *(Bows quickly, then, aside to* St. John) The Prince has gone mad! We must inform the King. *(To* Tom) A moment, Your Highness. *(*Hertford *and* St. John *exit rear.)*

Tom: Oh, there is no hope for me now. They will hang me for certain! *(*Hertford *and* St. John *re-enter, supporting* King. Tom *watches in awe as they help him to couch, where he sinks down wearily.)*

King *(Beckoning* Tom *close to him):* Now, my son, Edward, my prince. What is this? Do you mean to deceive me, the King, your father, who loves you and treats you so kindly?

Tom *(Dropping to his knees):* You are the King? Then I have no hope!

King *(Stunned):* My child, you are not well. Do not break your father's old heart. Say you know me.

Tom: Yes, you are my lord the King, whom God preserve.

King: True, that is right. Now, you will not deny that you are Prince of Wales, as they say you

BOWLING

did just a while ago?

TOM: I beg you, Your Grace, believe me. I am the lowest of your subjects, being born a pauper, and it is by a great mistake that I am here. I am too young to die. Oh, please, spare me, sire!

KING *(Amazed):* Die? Do not talk so, my child. You shall not die.

TOM *(Gratefully):* God save you, my king! And now, may I go?

KING: Go? Where would you go?

TOM: Back to the alley where I was born and bred to misery.

KING: My poor child, rest your head here. *(He holds TOM's head and pats his shoulder, then turns to HERTFORD and ST. JOHN.)* Alas, I am old and ill, and my son is mad. But this shall pass. Mad or sane, he is my heir and shall rule England. Tomorrow he shall be installed and confirmed in his princely dignity! Bring the Great Seal!

HERTFORD *(Bowing low):* Please, Your Majesty, you took the Great Seal from the Chancellor two days ago to give to His Highness the Prince.

KING: So I did. *(To TOM)* My child, tell me, where is the Great Seal?

TOM *(Trembling):* Indeed, my lord, I do not know.

KING: Ah, your affliction hangs heavily upon you. 'Tis no matter. You will remember later. Listen, carefully! *(Gently, but firmly)* I command you to hide your affliction in all ways that be within your power. You shall deny to no one that you are the true prince, and if your memory should fail you upon any occasion of state, you shall be advised by your uncle, the Lord Hertford.

TOM *(Resigned):* The King has spoken. The King shall be obeyed.

KING: And now, my child, I go to rest. *(He stands weakly, and HERTFORD leads him off, rear.)*

TOM (*Wearily, to* ST. JOHN): May it please your lordship to let me rest now?

ST. JOHN: So it please Your Highness, it is for you to command and us to obey. But it is wise that you rest, for this evening you must attend the Lord Mayor's banquet in your honor. (*He pulls bellcord, and* THREE PAGES *enter and kneel before* TOM.)

TOM: Banquet? (*Terrified, he sits on couch and reaches for cup of water, but* 1ST PAGE *instantly seizes cup, drops on one knee, and serves it to him.* TOM *starts to take off his boots, but* 2ND PAGE *stops him and does it for him. He tries to remove his cape and gloves, and* 3RD PAGE *does it for him.*) I wonder that you do not try to breathe for me also! (*Lies down cautiously.* PAGES *cover him with robe, then back away and exit.*)

ST. JOHN (*To* HERTFORD, *as he enters*): Plainly, what do you think?

HERTFORD: Plainly, this. The King is near death, my nephew the Prince of Wales is clearly mad and will mount the throne mad. God protect England, for she will need it!

ST. JOHN: Does it not seem strange that madness could so change his manner from what it used to be? It troubles me, his saying he is not the Prince.

HERTFORD: Peace, my lord! If he were an impostor and called himself Prince, that would be natural. But was there ever an impostor, who being called Prince by the King and court, denied it? Never! This is the true Prince gone mad. And tonight all London shall honor him. (HERTFORD *and* ST. JOHN *exit.* TOM *sits up, looks around helplessly, then gets up.*)

TOM: I should have thought to order something to eat. (*Sees bowl of nuts on table*) Ah! Here are some nuts! (*Looks around, sees Great Seal in armor, takes it out, looks at it curiously*) This will make a

good nutcracker. *(He takes bowl of nuts, sits on couch and begins to crack nuts with Great Seal and eat them, as curtain falls.)*

SCENE TWO

Time: *Later that night.*
Setting: *A street in London, near Offal Court. Played before the curtain.*
At Rise: PRINCE *limps in, dirty and tousled. He looks around wearily. Several* VILLAGERS *pass by, pushing against him.*

PRINCE: I have never seen this poor section of London. I must be near Offal Court. If I can only find it before I drop! *(*JOHN CANTY *steps out of crowd, seizes* PRINCE *roughly.)*

CANTY: Out at this time of night, and I warrant you haven't brought a farthing home! If that is the case and I do not break all the bones in your miserable body, then I am not John Canty!

PRINCE *(Eagerly):* Oh, are you his father?

CANTY: *His* father? I am *your* father, and—

PRINCE: Take me to the palace at once, and your son will be returned to you. The King, my father, will make you rich beyond your wildest dreams. Oh, save me, for I am indeed the Prince of Wales.

CANTY *(Staring in amazement):* Gone stark mad! But mad or not, I'll soon find where the soft places lie in your bones. Come home! *(Starts to drag* PRINCE *off)*

PRINCE *(Struggling):* Let me go! I am the Prince of Wales, and the King shall have your life for this!

CANTY *(Angrily):* I'll take no more of your madness! *(Raises stick to strike, but* PRINCE *struggles free and runs off, and* CANTY *runs after him.)*

Setting: *Same as Scene 1, with addition of dining table, set with dishes and goblets, on raised platform. Thronelike chair is at head of table.*
At Rise: *A banquet is in progress.* TOM, *in royal robes, sits at head of table, with* HERTFORD *at his right and* ST. JOHN *at his left.* LORDS *and* LADIES *sit around table eating and talking softly.*

TOM *(To* HERTFORD*):* What is this, my Lord? *(Holds up a plate)*
HERTFORD: Lettuce and turnips, Your Highness.
TOM: Lettuce and turnips? I have never seen them before. Am I to eat them?
HERTFORD *(Discreetly):* Yes, Your Highness, if you so desire. *(*TOM *begins to eat food with his fingers. Fanfare of trumpets is heard, and* HERALD *enters, carrying scroll. All turn to look.)*
HERALD *(Reading from scroll):* His Majesty, King Henry VIII, is dead! The King is dead! *(All rise and turn to* TOM, *who sits, stunned.)*
ALL *(Together):* The King is dead. Long live the King! Long live Edward, King of England! *(All bow to* TOM. HERALD *bows and exits.)*
HERTFORD *(To* TOM*):* Your Majesty, we must call the council. Come, St. John. *(*HERTFORD *and* ST. JOHN *lead* TOM *off at rear.* LORDS *and* LADIES *follow, talking among themselves. At gates, down right,* VILLAGERS *enter and mill about.* PRINCE *enters right, pounds on gates and shouts.)*
PRINCE: Open the gates! I am the Prince of Wales! Open, I say! And though I am friendless with no one to help me, I will not be driven from my ground.

MILES HENDON *(Entering through crowd):* Though you be Prince or not, you are indeed a gallant lad and not friendless. Here I stand to prove it, and you might have a worse friend than Miles Hendon.

1ST VILLAGER: 'Tis another prince in disguise. Take the lad and dunk him in the pond! *(He seizes* PRINCE, *but* MILES *strikes him with flat of his sword. Crowd, now angry, presses forward threateningly, when fanfare of trumpets is heard offstage.* HERALD, *carrying scroll, enters up left at gates.)*

HERALD: Make way for the King's messenger! *(Reading from scroll)* His Majesty, King Henry VIII, is dead! The King is dead! *(He exits right, repeating message, and* VILLAGERS *stand in stunned silence.)*

PRINCE *(Stunned):* The King is dead!

1ST VILLAGER *(Shouting):* Long live Edward, King of England!

VILLAGERS *(Together):* Long live the King! *(Shouting, ad lib)* Long live King Edward! Heaven protect Edward, King of England! *(Etc.)*

MILES *(Taking* PRINCE *by the arm):* Come, lad, before the crowd remembers us. I have a room at the inn, and you can stay there. *(He hurries off with stunned* PRINCE. TOM, *led by* HERTFORD, *enters courtyard up rear.* VILLAGERS *see them.)*

VILLAGERS *(Together):* Long live the King! *(They fall to their knees as curtains close.)*

SCENE FOUR

Setting: MILES's *room at the inn. At right is table set with dishes and bowls of food, a chair at each side. At left is bed, with table and chair next to it, and a window. Candle is on table.*

At Rise: MILES *and* PRINCE *approach table.*

MILES: I have had a hot supper prepared. I'll bet you're hungry, lad.

PRINCE: Yes, I am. It's kind of you to let me stay with you, Miles. I am truly Edward, King of England, and you shall not go unrewarded. *(Sits at table)*

MILES *(To himself)*: First he called himself Prince, and now he is King. Well, I will humor him. *(Starts to sit)*

PRINCE *(Angrily)*: Stop! Would you sit in the presence of the king?

MILES *(Surprised, standing up quickly)*: I beg your pardon, Your Majesty. I was not thinking. *(Stares uncertainly at PRINCE, who sits at table, expectantly. MILES starts to uncover dishes of food, serves PRINCE and fills glasses.)*

PRINCE: Miles, you have a gallant way about you. Are you nobly born?

MILES: My father is a baronet, Your Majesty.

PRINCE: Then you must also be a baronet.

MILES *(Shaking his head)*: My father banished me from home seven years ago, so I fought in the wars. I was taken prisoner, and I have spent the past seven years in prison. Now I am free, and I am returning home.

PRINCE: You have been shamefully wronged! But I will make things right for you. You have saved me from injury and possible death. Name your reward and if it be within the compass of my royal power, it is yours.

MILES *(Pausing briefly, then dropping to his knee)*: Since Your Majesty is pleased to hold my simple duty worthy of reward, I ask that I and my successors may hold the privilege of sitting in the presence of the King.

PRINCE *(Taking MILES's sword, tapping him lightly on each shoulder)*: Rise and seat yourself. *(Returns sword to MILES, then rises and goes over to bed)*

MILES (*Rising*): He should have been born a king. He plays the part to a marvel! If I had not thought of this favor, I might have had to stand for weeks. (*Sits down and begins to eat*)

PRINCE: Sir Miles, you will stand guard while I sleep. (*Lies down and instantly falls asleep*)

MILES: Yes, Your Majesty. (*With a rueful look at his uneaten supper, he stands up.*) Poor little chap. I suppose his mind has been disordered with ill usage. (*Covers* PRINCE *with his cape*) Well, I will be his friend and watch over him. (*Blows out candle, then yawns, sits on chair next to bed, and falls asleep.* JOHN CANTY *and* HUGO *appear at window, peer around room, then enter cautiously through window. They lift the sleeping* PRINCE, *staring nervously at* MILES.)

CANTY (*In loud whisper*): I swore the day he was born he would be a thief and a beggar, and I won't lose him now. Lead the way to the camp, Hugo! (CANTY *and* HUGO *carry* PRINCE *off right, as* MILES *sleeps on and curtain falls.*)

SCENE FIVE

Time: *Two weeks later.*
Setting: *Country village street.*
Before Rise: VILLAGERS *walk about.* CANTY, HUGO, *and* PRINCE *enter.*

CANTY: I will go in this direction. Hugo, keep my mad son with you, and see that he doesn't escape again! (*Exits*)

HUGO (*Seizing* PRINCE *by the arm*): He won't escape! I'll see that he earns his bread today, or else!

PRINCE (*Pulling away*): I will not beg with you, and I

will not steal! I have suffered enough in this miserable company of thieves!

HUGO: You shall suffer more if you do not do as I tell you! *(Raises clenched fist at PRINCE)* Refuse if you dare! *(WOMAN enters, carrying wrapped bundle in a basket on her arm.)* Wait here until I come back. *(HUGO sneaks along after WOMAN, then snatches her bundle, runs back to PRINCE, and thrusts it into his arms.)* Run after me and call, "Stop, thief!" But be sure you lead her astray! *(Runs off. PRINCE throws down bundle in disgust.)*

WOMAN: Help! Thief! Stop, thief! *(Rushes at PRINCE and seizes him, just as several VILLAGERS enter)* You little thief! What do you mean by robbing a poor woman? Somebody bring the constable! *(MILES enters and watches.)*

1ST VILLAGER *(Grabbing PRINCE):* I'll teach him a lesson, the little villain!

PRINCE *(Struggling):* Take your hands off me! I did not rob this woman!

MILES *(Stepping out of crowd and pushing man back with the flat of his sword):* Let us proceed gently, my friends. This is a matter for the law.

PRINCE *(Springing to MILES's side):* You have come just in time, Sir Miles. Carve this rabble to rags!

MILES: Speak softly. Trust in me and all shall go well.

CONSTABLE *(Entering and reaching for PRINCE):* Come along, young rascal!

MILES: Gently, good friend. He shall go peaceably to the Justice.

PRINCE: I will not go before a Justice! I did not do this thing!

MILES *(Taking him aside):* Sire, will you reject the laws of the realm, yet demand that your subjects respect them?

PRINCE *(Calmer):* You are right, Sir Miles. Whatever the King requires a subject to suffer under the law,

he will suffer himself while he holds the station of a subject. (CONSTABLE *leads them off right.* VILLAGERS *follow. Curtain*)

• • • • •

Setting: *Office of the Justice. A high bench is at center.*
At Rise: JUSTICE *sits behind bench.* CONSTABLE *enters with* MILES *and* PRINCE, *followed by* VILLAGERS. WOMAN *carries wrapped bundle.*

CONSTABLE *(To* JUSTICE*):* A young thief, your worship, is accused of stealing a dressed pig from this poor woman.

JUSTICE *(Looking down at* PRINCE, *then* WOMAN*):* My good woman, are you absolutely certain this lad stole your pig?

WOMAN: It was none other than he, your worship.

JUSTICE: Are there no witnesses to the contrary? *(All shake their heads.)* Then the lad stands convicted. *(To* WOMAN*)* What do you hold this property to be worth?

WOMAN: Three shillings and eight pence, your worship.

JUSTICE *(Leaning down to* WOMAN*):* Good woman, do you know that when one steals a thing above the value of thirteen pence, the law says he shall hang for it?

WOMAN *(Upset):* Oh, what have I done? I would not hang the poor boy for the whole world! Save me from this, your worship. What can I do?

JUSTICE *(Gravely):* You may revise the value, since it is not yet written in the record.

WOMAN: Then call the pig eight pence, your worship.

JUSTICE: So be it. You may take your property and go. *(WOMAN starts off, and is followed by* CONSTABLE. MILES *follows them cautiously down right.)*

CONSTABLE *(Stopping* WOMAN*):* Good woman, I will

buy your pig from you. *(Takes coins from pocket)* Here is eight pence.

WOMAN: Eight pence! It cost me three shillings and eight pence!

CONSTABLE: Indeed! Then come back before his worship and answer for this. The lad must hang!

WOMAN: No! No! Say no more. Give me the eight pence and hold your peace. *(CONSTABLE hands her coins and takes pig. WOMAN exits, angrily. MILES returns to bench.)*

JUSTICE: The boy is sentenced to a fortnight in the common jail. Take him away, Constable! *(JUSTICE exits. PRINCE gives MILES a nervous glance.)*

MILES *(Following CONSTABLE)*: Good sir, turn your back a moment and let the poor lad escape. He is innocent.

CONSTABLE *(Outraged)*: What? You say this to me? Sir, I arrest you in—

MILES: Do not be so hasty! *(Slyly)* The pig you have purchased for eight pence may cost you your neck, man.

CONSTABLE *(Laughing nervously)*: Ah, but I was merely jesting with the woman, sir.

MILES: Would the Justice think it a jest?

CONSTABLE: Good sir! The Justice has no more sympathy with a jest than a dead corpse! *(Perplexed)* Very well, I will turn my back and see nothing! But go quickly! *(Exits)*

MILES *(To PRINCE)*: Come, my liege. We are free to go. And that band of thieves shall not set hands on you again, I swear it!

PRINCE *(Wearily)*: Can you believe, Sir Miles, that in the last fortnight, I, the King of England, have escaped from thieves and begged for food on the road? I have slept in a barn with a calf! I have washed dishes in a peasant's kitchen, and narrowly escaped death. And not once in all my wanderings did I see a courier searching for me! Is it no matter for commotion and distress that the head of state is gone?

MILES *(Sadly, aside):* Still busy with his pathetic dream. *(To* PRINCE*)* It is strange indeed, my liege. But come, I will take you to my father's home in Kent. We are not far away. There you may rest in a house with seventy rooms! Come, I am all impatience to be home again! *(They exit,* MILES *in cheerful spirits,* PRINCE *looking puzzled, as curtains close.)*

SCENE SIX

Setting: *Village jail. Bare stage, with barred window on one wall.*
At Rise: TWO PRISONERS, *in chains, are onstage.* JAILER *shoves* MILES *and* PRINCE, *in chains, onstage. They struggle and protest.*

THEN
Before the 1700s, people were put in prison while awaiting trial and then punished publicly.

MILES: But I tell you I *am* Miles Hendon! My brother, Sir Hugh, has stolen my bride and my estate!

JAILER: Be silent! Impostor! Sir Hugh will see that you pay well for claiming to be his dead brother and for assaulting him in his own house! *(Exits)*

MILES *(Sitting, with head in hands):* Oh, my dear Edith . . . now wife to my brother Hugh, against her will, and my poor father . . . dead!

1ST PRISONER: At least you have your life, sir. I am sentenced to be hanged for killing a deer in the King's park.

2ND PRISONER: And I must hang for stealing a yard of cloth to dress my children.

PRINCE (*Moved; to* PRISONERS): When I mount my throne, you shall all be free. And the laws that have dishonored you shall be swept from the books. (*Turning away*) Kings should go to school to learn their own laws and be merciful.

1ST PRISONER: What does the lad mean? I have heard that the King is mad, but merciful.

2ND PRISONER: He is to be crowned at Westminster tomorrow.

PRINCE (*Violently*): King? What King, good sir?

1ST PRISONER: Why, we have only one, his most sacred majesty, King Edward the Sixth.

2ND PRISONER: And whether he be mad or not, his praises are on all men's lips. He has saved many innocent lives, and now he means to destroy the cruelest laws that oppress the people.

PRINCE (*Turning away, shaking his head*): How can this be? Surely it is not that little beggar boy!

(SIR HUGH *enters with* JAILER.)

SIR HUGH: Seize the impostor!

MILES (*As* JAILER *pulls him to his feet*): Hugh, this has gone far enough!

SIR HUGH: You will sit in the public stocks for two hours, and the boy would join you if he were not so young. See to it, jailer, and after two hours, you may release them. Meanwhile, I ride to London for the coronation! (SIR HUGH *exits and* MILES *is hustled out by* JAILER.)

PRINCE: Coronation! What does he mean? There can be no coronation without me! (*Curtain falls.*)

Time: *Coronation Day.*
Setting: *Outside gates of Westminster Abbey, played before curtain. Painted screen or flat at rear represents Abbey. Throne is center. Bench is near it.*
At Rise: LORDS *and* LADIES *crowd Abbey. Outside gates,* GUARDS *drive back cheering* VILLAGERS, *among them* MILES.

MILES: *(Distraught):* I've lost him! Poor little chap! He has been swallowed up in the crowd! *(Fanfare of trumpets is heard, then silence.* HERTFORD, ST. JOHN, LORDS *and* LADIES *enter slowly, in a procession, followed by* PAGES, *one of whom carries crown on small cushion.* TOM *follows procession, looking about nervously. Suddenly,* PRINCE, *in rags, steps out from crowd, his hand raised.)*

PRINCE: I forbid you to set the crown of England upon that head. I am the King!

HERTFORD: Seize the little vagabond!

TOM: I forbid it! He *is* the King! *(Kneels before* PRINCE*)* Oh, my lord the King, let poor Tom Canty be the first to say, "Put on your crown and enter into your own right again." *(*HERTFORD *and several* LORDS *look closely at both boys.)*

HERTFORD: This is strange indeed. *(To* TOM*)* By your favor, sir, I wish to ask certain questions of this lad.

PRINCE: I will answer truly whatever you may ask, my lord.

HERTFORD: But if you have been well trained, you may answer my questions as well as our lord the King. I need a definite proof. *(Thinks a moment)* Ah! Where lies the Great Seal of England? It has been missing for weeks, and only the true Prince of Wales can say where it lies.

TOM: Wait! Was the seal round and thick, with letters engraved on it? *(HERTFORD nods.)* I know where it is, but it was not I who put it there. The rightful King shall tell you. *(To PRINCE)* Think, my King, it was the very last thing you did that day before you rushed out of the palace wearing my rags.

PRINCE *(Pausing):* I recall how we exchanged clothes, but have no recollection of hiding the Great Seal.

TOM *(Eagerly):* Remember when you saw the bruise on my hand, you ran to the door, but first you hid this thing you call the Seal.

PRINCE *(Suddenly):* Ah! I remember! *(To ST. JOHN)* Go, my good St. John, and you shall find the Great Seal in the armor that hangs on the wall in my chamber. *(ST. JOHN hesitates, but at a nod from TOM, hurries off.)*

TOM *(Pleased):* Right, my King! Now the scepter of England is yours again. *(ST. JOHN returns in a moment with Great Seal.)*

ALL *(Shouting):* Long live Edward, King of England! *(TOM takes off his cape and throws it over PRINCE's rags. Trumpet fanfare is heard. ST. JOHN takes crown and places it on PRINCE. All kneel.)*

HERTFORD: Let the small imposter be flung into the Tower!

PRINCE *(Firmly):* I will not have it so. But for him, I would not have my crown. *(To TOM)* My poor boy, how was it that you could remember where I hid the Seal, when I could not?

TOM *(Embarrassed):* I did not know what it was, my King, and I used it to . . . to crack nuts. *(All laugh, and TOM steps back. MILES steps forward, staring in amazement.)*

MILES: Is he really the King? Is he indeed the sovereign

of England, and not the poor and friendless Tom o' Bedlam I thought he was? *(He sinks down on bench.)* I wish I had a bag to hide my head in!

1ST GUARD *(Rushing up to him):* Stand up, you mannerless clown! How dare you sit in the presence of the King!

PRINCE: Do not touch him! He is my trusty servant, Miles Hendon, who saved me from shame and possible death. For his service, he owns the right to sit in my presence.

MILES *(Bowing, then kneeling):* Your Majesty!

PRINCE: Rise, Sir Miles. I command that Sir Hugh Hendon, who sits within this hall, be seized and put under lock and key until I have need of him. *(Beckons to* TOM*)* From what I have heard, Tom Canty, you have governed the realm with royal gentleness and mercy in my absence. Henceforth, you shall hold the honorable title of King's Ward! *(*TOM *kneels and kisses* PRINCE's *hand.)* And because I have suffered with the poorest of my subjects and felt the cruel force of unjust laws, I pledge myself to a reign of mercy for all! *(All bow low, then rise.)*

ALL *(Shouting):* Long live the King! Long live Edward, King of England! *(Curtain)*

The End

THINKING ABOUT IT

1 If this were a play about *you*, with whom would you trade places? Why? What would be the title?

2 Here's a TV ad to get people to come to this play: *The Prince and the Pauper* contains comedy, adventure, and a serious message at the end—all three in just one play! Use the script of the play to support those extravagant claims.

3 Some modern play productions do not use scenery or costumes. If you produced this play without scenery or costumes, how could you show when it happened? How could you make the action clear?

Another Book by Mark Twain

In *A Connecticut Yankee in King Arthur's Court,* a nineteenth-century Yankee wakes up in King Arthur's Court and works to bring about reforms.

PEOPLE

of the Four

QUARTERS

By Ritva Lehtinen

Photographs by Matti A. Pitkänen

There is a legend that long ago the sun sent two of his children to earth to start a new civilization. It is said that the brother and sister rose out of the waters of Lake Titicaca, high in the Andes Mountains of South America. They settled in the Cuzco Valley in what would one day be Peru. This was the beginning of a great people that would come to be known as the Incas.

Whether or not you believe this legend, it is probably true that the Inca Empire grew out of a small group of people who lived in the Cuzco Valley. By the 1500s, this civilization numbered over 10 million people, and it included parts of what is now Peru, Bolivia, Colombia, Argentina, Ecuador, and Chile.

The Inca Empire disappeared long ago. But many of the people who now live in and around the Andes Mountains are descendants of the Incas. The people that are most often identified with their Incan ancestors are the Quechua Indians. These are the people we will call "the grandchildren of the Incas."

The Inca Empire was ruled by an emperor, who was called the Lord Inca. The Lord Inca made sure that everyone had food, clothing, shelter, and medical care. In exchange, the people were expected to work hard and follow strict laws.

While the common people lived quite simply, the Lord Inca and his nobles lived in luxury. They wore clothes embroidered with gold and silver, and they ate from golden dishes.

The Inca Empire grew rapidly. The Incas conquered surrounding peoples, taking over their land and sometimes adopting their ways. But in the 1530s, the Incas themselves were conquered by the Spanish. Soon there was very little left of the Incan civilization. The Spanish stole its treasures, destroyed its cities, and made its people slaves.

The people we know as the Incas called themselves "the People of the Four Quarters." They used the word *Inca* to describe their leader and his nobles. But the Spanish thought that all of the People of the Four Quarters were called Incas. So in modern times, *Inca* refers to everyone who made up the Inca Empire.

Most modern Quechua Indians live in the mountains of Peru and Bolivia. Tomás and José live in Peru, near the village of Urubamba. For hundreds of years, their ancestors have farmed the mountain soil.

The Incas used advanced farming methods that made it possible for them to grow crops on steep, rocky land and in places where rain seldom fell. They farmed the steep slopes by building giant steps, called terraces, into the mountainside. They used pipes and channels to bring water from rivers and lakes to their fields.

Most of the Quechua still make their living by farming. Like their Incan ancestors, they grow such

crops as potatoes, corn, a root vegetable called oca, and a grain called quinoa. Some people still use the terraces built by the Incas long ago.

Carmen, her mother, and her brothers are herding sheep on the ruins of Tambomachay near Cuzco. Carmen is holding the lamb her parents gave her for her sixth birthday. She knows she must take good care of the lamb because her family needs its wool to make into clothes.

Carmen's mother is spinning wool into yarn. When she's done, she'll use the yarn to knit a warm sweater. She hopes to sell the sweater in town to make a little extra money.

Sheep are not the only animals herded by the Quechua. Some people raise llamas or alpacas. Both llamas and alpacas are large, woolly animals that are related to the camel. These exotic creatures are very useful to the Quechua. Their wool can be used to make clothing, and their hides can be made into leather. Llama and alpaca meat can be eaten, and even their manure can be dried and burned as fuel.

THEN The ransom for an Incan emperor captured in 1532 was a room filled with gold and another filled twice with silver.

Like the Quechua, the Incas who lived in the mountains raised llamas and alpacas. Until the 1500s, the Incas had never seen a cow, horse, sheep, or ox. These animals, along with many others, were brought to South America by the Spanish.

Llamas were very important to the Incas, who considered them to be sacred. Sometimes llamas were sacrificed to the gods in special ceremonies. The Incas worshipped several gods, including Inti—the sun god—and Viracocha—the creator.

Llamas provided the Incas with food, clothing, fuel, and even transportation. They could carry heavy loads and, like camels, were able to go long periods of time without water. This made them ideal pack animals. Cart-pulling bicycles and small trucks have only recently started to take their place on the steep paths of the Andes Mountains.

Weaving is a skill that has been passed down from the Incas to the modern Quechua Indians. The Indians' work is known for its bright colors and eye-catching patterns. The material is as warm and durable as it is beautiful.

The Quechua wear both modern and traditional clothing—often at the same time. Many of the traditional clothes they wear have changed very little since the time of the Incas.

One popular item of clothing worn by Quechuan men that was also worn by the Incas is the poncho. A poncho is a large piece of heavy material with a slit in the middle to go over the wearer's head. It is very warm and takes the place of a coat.

Like her Incan ancestors, a Quechuan woman might wear a large multicolored shawl instead of a poncho. The shawl is useful for carrying packages and also provides a warm, safe way to carry a baby.

It is rare to see a Quechua Indian, young or old, without a hat. The men and children usually wear knitted caps with warm earflaps. Some of the women wear bowler hats, with turned-up brims; others wear beautifully patterned hats.

Cuzco was not only the Incas' first settlement, it was also their capital city and the home of their leader.

Before Cuzco was taken by the Spanish, it was a lively city of more than 100,000 people. Its palaces and temples were covered with gold and filled with priceless treasures.

Now the treasures are gone and so are many of the Incas' buildings. But here and there, parts of the original city have survived. Some of Cuzco's buildings are

Peru is one of four major sources of silver in the world—the others are Canada, Mexico, and Britain.

N O W

built on the foundations of Incan ruins. Walls built by the Incas line the narrow streets of the oldest parts of the city. And most of the people who live in Cuzco are descendants of the Incas.

The Incas built their largest structures—their walls, palaces, temples, and fortresses—out of giant stones. The Incan stonemasons fit the stones together so closely that no mortar was needed. The stones held each other in place just like the pieces of a jigsaw puzzle.

The Incas' roads were as well constructed as their buildings. Two major roads crossed the Inca Empire. One cut through the mountains, and the other traveled along the coast. These two roads were connected by smaller roads that ran between them. Altogether, the Incan roads covered about 10,000 miles.

The Incas were such skillful builders that, despite wars and earthquakes, many of their structures are still standing, and some of the roads they built are still in use.

THINKING ABOUT IT

1 You are a tour director. What feature of the Incas, past or present, would you describe to a group of tourists to prepare them for a tour of the land of the Incas? Tell why you would choose to tell them about that feature.

2 Some people glance at photographs. Some people study them. Select one photograph in this article about the Incas. Examine it closely. Then, without looking at it again, tell what you saw in it as if you had been there.

3 Suppose you are going to live for a week with a Quechua Indian family. What would you ask about the visit before you go?

Another Book About the Incas

In *Lost City in the Clouds: The Discovery of Machu Picchu,* Elizabeth Gemming tells about Hiram Bingham's discovery of the lost city of the Incas.

The
GOLD
of West Africa

By Mary Daniels

All the fables of golden treasure, from Incan
El Dorado to Yukon gold strikes, are mere glitter
when compared to the story of the dazzling gold of
Africa.

The history of the great empires of Africa and the
way that these empires have influenced the world since
ancient times can be told through the story of gold.
For some fifteen hundred years, the gold fields of West
Africa have produced enough gold to adorn kings,
chiefs, and common people. For centuries gold was
widely traded, both as jewelry and as gold dust.

One of the most famous of the early rulers was the
Emperor Mansa Musa who reigned from 1312 to 1337
over the great West African empire of Mali, an area as
large as France and Spain combined. In 1324 Mansa
Musa succeeded in making the wealth of Mali known

The most common Baule beads are disks and rectangles.

to the outside world when he made a religious pilgrimage to Mecca, taking with him an entourage of 60,000 people. His caravans included thousands of slaves carrying bars of gold and hundreds of camels burdened with bags of gold dust. Imagine his dazzling presence in Cairo!

Accounts of African kings of the past and the present, adorned for special public occasions, make the myth of King Midas appear to have come true. Picture heavy gold necklaces and pendants, finger rings in the shape of twisted knots or various animals, massive bracelets carved of wood and covered with gold leaf for the arms, and bands for elbows and ankles. Sandals and crowns were ornamented with gold. Sometimes even beards were threaded with gold beads.

While the gold fields were exploited from the fourth century A.D., it was only after the fifteenth century that the West African areas were influenced by trade with European countries. Merchant traders from countries such as Portugal, England, and France reported that people on the West African coast wore lavish gold ornaments and often traded them for products made in Europe. Gold dust and bullion were exported, and European kings used coins made of West African gold.

Few older pieces have survived to the present day due to the practice of recycling, or reusing, gold by melting it down and recasting it. Because gold is so valuable, people sell or trade it in times of need, or they have it recast into more fashionable ornaments as styles change. Most jewelry from West Africa dates back only to the nineteenth and twentieth centuries.

These chiefs' leather sandals, with ornaments of carved wood and gold, come from the Akan region of Ghana.

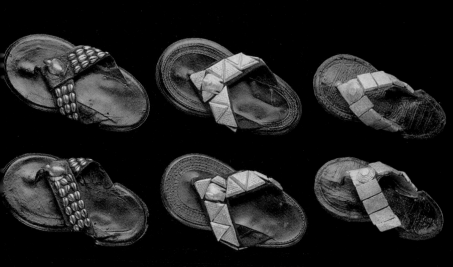

Leonardo

DA VINCI

By Robert Gardner

For centuries the world has regarded Leonardo da Vinci (1452–1519) as one of the world's greatest painters. The faces we see in his *Mona Lisa* and *Last Supper* are amazingly real. Leonardo's notebooks, discovered in this century in old libraries, reveal that Leonardo was more than a great painter. He was an inventor, architect, botanist, ecologist, astronomer, mathematician, and anatomist.

Unfortunately for the world, Leonardo kept his ideas to himself. His notebooks are written in print that can be read only with a mirror. Did he fear the wrath of other scholars who held different opinions? Or was he keeping his findings secret until that day when he would at last understand the grand design of nature?

We now doubt he wrote in mirror image form in order to keep his ideas secret. Rather, because he was left-handed he probably found it easier to write from right to left.

His inventions, which were drawn in great detail in his notebooks, were often centuries ahead of their time. For example, he invented a four-wheel horseless wagon powered by two giant springs that were to be alternately wound by a "conductor" using a lever. Recognizing that wheels would have to turn at different speeds on curves, he circumvented the need for a differential by supplying power to only one wheel. His car was the forerunner of today's toy wind-up cars. Why don't we find spring-powered cars on today's highways?

He invented a wooden tank for warfare. The tank, made of heavy planks, had a cannon on each side, in front, and in back. It was mounted on four wheels powered by cranks turned by men inside. He invented

a diving suit that would allow a diver to breathe air stored in a wineskin as he made his way to the bottom of the hull of an enemy ship. Once there, he could cut holes in the ship causing it to sink.

Some of his other inventions include a movable cam, a ratchet jack, a device for measuring the strength of wires, a machine for rolling copper and tin into sheets, a monkey wrench, a pair of pliers, a reciprocating saw, a pipe borer, a device for automatically feeding paper into printing presses, a needle grinder to mass-produce needles, a pedometer, a machine for stamping coins, a device for measuring wind speed, a worm gear, a pump to force water from deep wells or mines, a floating dredge to clear swamps, and a type of prefabricated housing. He developed cord drives. In his notebook he wrote, "Every motion machine with cords is quieter than one that is made with toothed wheels and pinions." He thus anticipated today's belt-driven machines. Da Vinci was surely an inventor ahead of his time!

He was a man of opposites. He despised war and spoke of it as "bestial madness," but served Cesare Borgia as an engineer during Borgia's military campaigns in 1502. Though he bought caged birds in order to set them free and refused to eat flesh because he opposed the killing of animals, he designed automatic spits powered by falling weights to roast meat. He painted the *Mona Lisa* and the *Last Supper,* but also sketched the gory details of war and hangings. He seemed to be fascinated by the extremes inherent in human nature.

Leonardo's Style of Inventing

For Leonardo, nature held all the great designs. His intense curiosity led him to conduct careful observations and investigations as he attempted to understand nature's grand plan. To design airplanes, he studied birds in flight. To design submarines, he watched fish as they swam. He sought to design machines that functioned as efficiently and automatically as the living bodies found in nature. Leonardo saw a machine as a living body—a series of parts, all working together. He recognized that though a machine might consist of gears, pulleys, belts, chains, screws, levers, connecting rods, cams, ratchets, and other parts, as a whole it was more than the sum of its parts. Like so many inventors, Leonardo was able to find similarities or likenesses among things and ideas that for most people were totally unrelated.

THEN

Ornithopters were flying machines first sketched by da Vinci.

To better understand the working and structure of the human body, he dissected cadavers, drawing detailed sketches of what he saw, including the heart and its internal structure. His notes reveal that he wondered how the heart might be made to work better, for Leonardo was a perfectionist. He was never satisfied with his inventions or his paintings. He would come back to them and see ways to improve them. His notebooks contained dozens of ways to convert reciprocating (back-and-forth) motion to rotary motion and vice versa—work that preceded similar efforts by James Watt to build a steam engine by 300 years.

In 1986, Richard Rutan and Jeana Yeager flew nonstop around the world at the record speed of 115.65 mph.

N O W

With time Leonardo would always see ways to improve everything he invented. So, in a sense, he never finished anything. His perfectionism prevented him from feeling that he had ever really succeeded. His curiosity about everything constantly distracted him from one investigation to another. He lacked Thomas Edison's perseverance because his interests were far broader. He had no great desire to make money. He sought to understand the grand scheme of the universe, not the solution to a single pressing problem.

Above all, Leonardo's style was visual. He had a superb ability to observe and to see every detail in the things he viewed. This is evident in his paintings where we see every line, every eyelash, every detail in the subject's expression. His uncanny eye for detail enabled him to see each and every flaw in his paintings. A century before Galileo showed that a projectile follows a parabolic (curved) path, Leonardo's sharp eye enabled him to see and sketch the paths of cannon balls. He knew they did not rise and then suddenly fall, as many believed.

His keen vision was coupled with a vast imagination and an outstanding ability to visualize. In his mind he could "see" the solution to problems and then transfer his mental images onto paper. Beside his drawings he would write detailed operating directions. His ability to coordinate hand, eye, and mind to visualize a better solution to a problem for which he had devised an invention has probably never been equaled.

His style can also be characterized as scientific. His artistic eye for detail led him to the realization that details are important in understanding nature as well. We cannot understand nature or solve problems solely by reasoning from general principles. His studies led him to understand that many of the established principles about nature, as stated by the scholars of his day, were false. He recognized that generalizations about nature could be made only by finding common threads among a large number of specific examples (called "inductive reasoning"). Given enough specific observations, we may find a common principle that explains all the individual details.

THINKING ABOUT IT

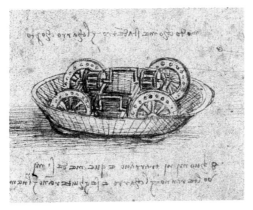

1   "The gold of West Africa? I've never heard about it." If someone says this to you, what can you tell that person about West African gold?

2   The author states that Leonardo was "centuries ahead of his time." Use the article about him to support or to argue against that judgment.

3   If Leonardo da Vinci were living now instead of 1452–1519, what would he be doing? Make a list that might attract his interest.

HATS

to Believe In

By Margaret Cooper

When he was ten years old, the hero of a story set in India remembers, his father took him to the mosque to celebrate a Muslim holiday "by tying a handkerchief over my head and pressing my forehead to the ground." A handkerchief is not much of a hat: It gives little shelter from sun, rain, or cold and certainly will not win any fashion prizes. But in principle, it covers the head.

Many Muslim men entering a mosque cover their heads out of respect for God in the place of prayer. Whether a handkerchief or a more recognized hat such as a fez or a turban, Muslim hats leave the forehead bare so that it can touch the ground, as our hero reports, when the kneeling man bows in prayer.

Out of respect for God, some Jewish men wear a hat at all times, in the house and outdoors. Most famil- iar is the *yarmulke,* usually a plain, black skullcap. Young men sometimes wear a small, crocheted yarmulke, which might be a plain, subdued color or patterned. Like the handkerchief, it covers the head symbolically.

Christian men believe that respect for God means *un*covering the head. If a Christian man is wearing a hat when he enters a church, he removes it. On the other hand, some Christian women will do just the opposite, covering their heads with a scarf—or even that useful handkerchief—when they enter a church.

Traditionally, going to weekly church service calls for wearing your "Sunday best" hat, and on Easter Sunday, the grand, new Easter bonnets with their ribbons and other finery signal the renewal of life for which Easter stands.

Putting on a hat or taking it off is one way to show your belief. Wearing a particular kind of head covering is another. All women, even very young girls, of the Hutterite sect in Canada wear a patterned scarf tied under the chin. Men who belong to the Amish sect wear broad-brimmed, black hats as they go about their work, farming the rich land of eastern Pennsylvania. A somewhat similar hat is worn by men in communities of very orthodox Chassidic Jews, which flourish in several Brooklyn neighborhoods. People of all these sects originally lived in Europe. When they migrated across the ocean, they brought with them their traditional faith and the traditional clothing that proclaimed

it. Like military uniforms, what they wear is a bond among members of the group and informs others who they are.

Across the world in India, orthodox men of the Sikh faith also wear a hat at all times. Their hat is a turban wound in a special way. Out of respect for the gurus, or teachers, who founded their religion centuries ago, Sikhs do not cut their hair, but roll it, knot it at the end, and tuck it under the turban. When they leave their homeland for other parts of the world, they continue wearing the hat connected with their religious belief. It is common to see turbaned Sikhs walking on the streets of large cities such as New York. In London, where many have settled, if a Sikh works at a public job such as driving a city bus, he may wear his turban on the job with his bus driver's uniform.

The color of a hat may also have a special meaning. A white and gold turban worn by a Muslim man shows that he has made a pilgrimage to Mecca, while a green turban may be worn only by men in the family line of Mohammed, founder of the Muslim religion. Hat color counts with certain orders of the Buddhist religion, too. Monks of the Yellow Hat sect in Tibet, high in the Himalaya Mountains, traditionally followed beliefs a little different from those of Black Hat monks.

THEN

As hats on the head became more pointed through the 15th century, so did the toes of shoes, extending up to 24 inches.

In the Catholic Church, the red *biretta* is reserved for cardinals, next in importance to the pope. The choice of the color red dates to the time of the Crusades in medieval Europe, when Christians fought the Muslims to reclaim the Holy Land. Wearing a red hat showed that the cardinals were willing to shed blood for their beliefs. The pope himself has a crown comparable to crowns worn by European kings. As the king—or sometimes the queen—at one time had authority over worldly affairs, so the pope guides the followers of his faith.

Colorful religious hats, as with colorful plumage in birds, usually are worn by the male of the species. While some Christian women have their gay Easter bonnets, the women of most other major faiths are likely to cover their heads with a plain shawl or veil. It is often black.

In tribal life, wearing the proper headdress can give

a priest or other special people the power to reach out to spirits whose help is needed. The headdress, often masking the whole head, helps transform the person wearing it. To attract or perhaps even take on the spirits of the buffalo, Plains Indian buffalo dancers wore such a headdress. Made of buffalo skin and horns, it resembled the buffalo's head. A famous Ice Age painting in a French cave shows a dancing figure who could be the remote "ancestor" of the buffalo dancers. His head is covered by a bearded animal mask topped with antlers. Like the buffalo dancers, he also wears a cape of animal skin with the tail trailing down. We might guess that he represents a shaman (priest) performing a hunting ceremony thirteen thousand years ago.

Not too far from where the buffalo used to roam, Hopi Indian farmers sometimes wear stepped "cloud" headdresses in ceremonies to bring the rain needed for their crops. Bambara farmers in Mali, West Africa, have a yearly harvest celebration honoring the mythical ancestor, half man and half antelope, believed to have taught them how to grow grain. The dancers wear a headdress crowned with a beautifully carved wooden antelope and sometimes leap into the air, antelope fashion, to show how high next year's grain will grow. And far away on the South Pacific island of New Britain, dancers wear enormous bark hats decorated with flowers, feathers, and other ornaments to bring good will from the weather spirits.

Special headdresses are also chosen for ceremonies that relate to important life events, such as passing from childhood to adulthood. For instance, a leopardskin hat worn by the priest of an African forest group is meant to help boys going through the initiation ceremony take on the strength of the leopard.

Manufacturers are finding ways to cushion sneakers by pumping air into them.

N O W

The gods, too, sometimes wear hats that show their place in the heavenly realm. The winged helmet of Hermes symbolized his speed in carrying messages for the other ancient Greek gods. Isis, ancient Egyptian goddess of the heavens, wore a solar disk flanked by cow horns. (Originally, the cow represented heaven, with its four legs serving as pillars to the sky.) The two Egyptian gods of the Nile wore crowns, one of lotus and the other of papyrus, two plants that grow in the Nile and were much valued by the Egyptians.

In modern West Africa, Shango, thunder god of the Yoruba people, wears a hat bearing a double ax, his powerful thunder symbol. The voodoo gods of Haiti carry on West African traditions, but New World costumes influence what they wear. For example, Zaka, god of agriculture, dresses like a peasant in a big straw hat and blue smock. You can see the most hats in India on the demon-king Ravana, an evil spirit in the Hindu epic of Prince Rama. Every one of Ravana's ten wicked heads has a crown.

THINKING ABOUT IT

1 What interesting or unusual hats do you remember wearing or seeing? Describe a hat that stands out in your memory and tell why it is so memorable.

2 "Hats to Believe In"—how do hats show the beliefs of the people who wear them? Since there are so many kinds of hats, why is *universal* a good word to describe hats? Use examples from the selection.

3 Design a hat yourself. What is its shape? Its color? Would you wear it all the time, or only on certain occasions? What does your hat tell others about YOU?

18

Entrada de
Cortes En Me
xico. Por la Cal
sada de S. Anto
nio Abad.

18

The
WONDER
WORKER

By Suzanne Jurmain

The year was 1524. General Hernando Cortez, the famed Spanish conqueror of Mexico, was leading a troop of soldiers through Guatemala when his warhorse, Morzillo, suddenly started to limp. Examination showed a long, sharp splinter had pierced the animal's foot. Healing would take days, and the general was in a hurry. Since he couldn't wait for the horse to recover, Cortez asked residents of the nearby town of Tayascal to look after Morzillo until he returned.

The startled Indians agreed to do their best, but they really didn't know where to begin. None of them had ever seen a horse before, and the big black four-legged thing looked dangerous. Finally they decided to treat Morzillo like a king.

Servants kept the horse's manger full of fresh flowers, succulent fruit, and roast fowl. But this rich, exotic diet only made Morzillo sicker, and one dreadful day the poor horse died.

The distraught Indians couldn't replace the stallion, so they decided to give Cortez a statue of his horse instead. The finished sculpture was placed in a temple for safekeeping, and the Indians waited for the general to return.

He never did, and the statue of Morzillo never left the temple. As the years passed, old men showed it to their children and their grandchildren. Storytellers told fabulous tales about this amazing four-legged animal, and soon legends about Morzillo's magic powers began to circulate through the neighborhood.

One hundred years after Cortez's visit, two Catholic friars made their way to Tayascal. They walked into the town's largest temple and stared. There in front of them was a statue of a horse sitting on its haunches. Offerings of fruit and flowers surrounded the image and Indians prayed to it, calling it Tziminchac, lord of thunder. In one short century Morzillo, the lame Spanish war-horse, had become a god.

These events actually took place in a little sixteenth-century Guatemalan town, but they could just as easily have occurred in Europe, Asia, or North Africa before the beginning of the modern scientific era. In those bygone centuries many men and women truly believed that horses could be gods, magicians, and miracle workers. Stories about horses with strange supernatural powers were told in almost every country, and it's easy to understand why. To people who lived before the machine age, a real horse seemed like a fairy-tale creature. It was swift, strong, and beautiful, and it had the power to whisk a traveler to the ends of the earth, bring a warrior victory, feed a family, or help a poor worker make a fortune. To these basic facts, storytellers added a touch of imagination. Then, from this new mixture of fact and fantasy, they wove fabulous tales about magical horses that performed miracles, changed the lives of individuals, and controlled the forces of nature.

Nothing on earth moves faster than time, water, and weather, and the ancients imagined that swift, wonder-working horses helped regulate all three. In those early days many people thought galloping horses carried the life-giving sun across the sky in the daytime, and some believed magical steeds pulled the moon through the heavens at night. Twenty-seven hundred years ago Greeks claimed that Poseidon, the sea god who often appeared in the form of a horse, created the earth's fresh-flowing rivers and streams. Across the world in ancient India men and women pointed at the scudding rain clouds and said that fierce storm spirits called the Maruts were driving their horse-drawn chariots across the sky. In more recent times Czechs sang about a white horse that brought the winter's snow, and storytellers from certain parts of Russia and central Asia claimed the calendar itself ran on horsepower. Up in the sky, they said, lived a certain magic horse. Year in and year out, he paced around the North Star, pulling the wheel of the seasons, changing summer to autumn and winter to spring.

Sun steeds and storm steeds helped make the land fertile, and so did other horses. Long before the horse became a regular farmhand, men and women apparently thought this strong, energetic animal possessed a life-giving force that made plants grow and animals flourish. The belief was widespread, and people expressed it in different ways. In one part of ancient Greece worshippers prayed before a statue of the harvest goddess, Demeter, that had a woman's body and a horse's head. Old Chinese and Japanese myths say that the first silkworms hatched out of the hide of a dead stallion. Until the nineteenth century farmers in parts of England, France, and Germany thought the corn spirit, a genie that made plants grow, traveled from field to field in the form of a mare. And by about 700–600 B.C. Romans were using horse magic to grow crops.

In those early centuries Rome wasn't the hub of a mighty empire. It was a sleepy little market town nestled among seven green hills on the banks of the Tiber River. Most of its citizens were farmers, and each year on October 15 they left their fields to attend the season's most important agricultural rite, a chariot race.

The race, which was held on the king's fields outside the city, was a fairly ordinary contest, but there was nothing ordinary about the prize. At the finish a priest stabbed one of the victorious chariot horses with a spear, sacrificing it to Mars, the god of war and harvests. Blood from the unlucky victim's body was carefully siphoned into a bottle and later used to purify livestock so the herds would thrive. The horse's tail was carried to the king's house so it could bring health and prosperity to the ruler and the nation. Finally the animal's head was cut off, nailed to a wall, and decorated with a string of loaves so that it would bring Roman farmers a bountiful harvest.

THEN
About 1728 three horses were brought to England from the Near East.

Historians say that humans tamed the horse, but legends say horses helped tame humans. According to the myths, horselike gods and godlike horses provided people with many of the basic elements of civilization. Back at the beginning of time, Chinese storytellers said, a dragon-headed horse brought the legendary emperor Fu-Hsi eight mystic symbols, eight magic keys to the secrets of philosophy, religion, and prophecy. Ancient Greeks told their children about Chiron the Centaur, a wise creature, half man and half horse, who educated the mightiest heroes and taught medicine to the god of healing. Indian mythmakers said that the god Vishnu preserved religious knowledge by donning a horse's head and rescuing the sacred Hindu scriptures from a pair of demons. Romans even claimed that literature owed a lot to Pegasus, a flying horse, who was said to have created the Hippocrene, a sacred fountain that inspired poets to write great verse.

In addition to giving horses credit for providing the human race with everything from artistic inspiration to medical knowledge, storytellers claimed that some wonder-working horses changed history. In Italy the ancients believed that two magic white steeds, ridden by the demigods Castor and Pollux, swooped down from heaven and helped a hard-pressed Roman army win the battle of Lake Regillus in 496 B.C.

The three horses are ancestors of nearly every thoroughbred in training today.

N O W

Sensible historians may think architects and engineers helped Emperor Ch'in Shih Huang Ti choose the site of the Great Wall of China, but legends say a wonder-working white horse led construction crews across northern Asia and marked the perfect building location with its hoof-prints. Czechs once thought a magic horse chose one of their greatest medieval kings. And in the Near East devout Moslems say that no one paid attention to the words of the religious leader Muhammad (A.D. 570–632) until a winged horse named al-Borak took the unsuccessful prophet on a round-trip ride to heaven for a midnight conference with God.

All these legendary horses were powerful, and all were white. The gods sometimes confided in white horses, heroes rode them, and storytellers often described their magical feats.

But not all horse magicians were white. Until recently men and women in certain parts of rural England believed that a piebald horse could grant a wish if a person walked up to it and said:

> *Black's white and white's black*
> *Over the nag's back.*
> *Make my wish come true, wish come true*
> *Wish come very very true.*

Eastern European storytellers described another powerful group of horse magicians. In olden times Russian families often huddled around the stove on snowy nights and listened to a tale that began with these words: "Once upon a time, a very long time ago, there lived a poor young peasant named Ivan. He had no money and no land. But he did have one precious possession: a little hunchback horse with magic powers." Then the narrator explained how the little horse carried Ivan to the ends of the earth, saved him from the clutches of an evil king, arranged for him to marry a beautiful princess, and finally helped the young man to win a royal crown.

Today the story of the little hunchback horse is famous, but it is not unique. Dozens of other folk tales also chronicle the adventures of old, sick, lame, or misshapen horses that use magic powers to help human heroes win fame and fortune.

THINKING ABOUT IT

1. "Horses no longer fascinate people as they once did." Do you agree or disagree with this statement? Explain.

2. "The Wonder-Worker" is called nonfiction, even though much of its horse lore can't be true. Explain, then, why it is called nonfiction.

3. An article like this one seems to present ideas from all over the world. Instead of writing these tidbits from here and there, how else could you present them in order to celebrate horse lore in history?

A Book About Horses Through History

Did you know that horses were important characters in history? Read more about how horses helped humans change the world in *Once Upon a Horse* by Suzanne Jurmain.

FIRST GLIMPSE

From "The Witch of Blackbird Pond"

By Elizabeth George Speare

On a morning in mid-April, 1687, the brigantine
Dolphin left the open sea, sailed briskly across the
Sound to the wide mouth of the Connecticut River and
into Saybrook harbor. Kit Tyler had been on the fore-
castle deck since daybreak, standing close to the rail,
staring hungrily at the first sight of land for five weeks.

"There's Connecticut Colony," a voice spoke in
her ear. "You've come a long way to see it."

She looked up, surprised and flattered. On the
whole long voyage the captain's son had spoken
scarcely a dozen words to her. She had noticed him
often, his thin wiry figure swinging easily hand over
hand up the rigging, his sandy, sun-bleached head bent
over a coil of rope. Nathaniel Eaton, first mate, but his
mother called him Nat. Now, seeing him so close
beside her, she was surprised that, for all he looked so
slight, the top of her head barely reached his shoulder.

"How does it look to you?" he questioned.

Kit hesitated. She didn't want to admit how disappointing she found this first glimpse of America. The bleak line of shore surrounding the gray harbor was a disheartening contrast to the shimmering green and white that fringed the turquoise bay of Barbados which was her home. The earthen wall of the fortification that faced the river was bare and ugly, and the houses beyond were no more than plain wooden boxes.

"Is that Wethersfield?" she inquired instead.

"Oh, no, Wethersfield is some way up the river. This is the port of Saybrook. Home to us Eatons. There's my father's shipyard, just beyond the dock."

She could just make out the row of unimpressive shacks and the flash of raw new lumber. Her smile was admiring from pure relief. At least this grim place was not her destination, and surely the colony at Wethersfield would prove more inviting.

THEN
In 1700, most ships carried cargo or were used as warships.

"We've made good time this year," Nat went on. "It's been a fair passage, hasn't it?"

"Oh, yes," she sparkled. "Though I'm glad now 'tis over."

"Aye," he agreed. "I never know myself which is best, the setting out or the coming back to harbor. Ever been on a ship before?"

"Just the little pinnaces in the islands. I've sailed on those all my life."

He nodded. "That's where you learned to keep your balance."

So he had noticed! To her pride, she had proved to be a natural sailor. Certainly she had not spent the voyage groaning and retching like some of the passengers.

"You're not afraid of the wind and the salt, anyway. At least, you haven't spent much time below."

"Not if I could help it," she laughed. Did he think anyone would stay in that stuffy cabin by choice? Would she ever have had the courage to sail at all had she known, before she booked passage, that the sugar and molasses in the hold had been paid for by a load of Connecticut horses, and that all the winds of the Atlantic could never blow the ship clean of that unbearable stench? "That's what I minded most about the storm," she added, "four days shut away down there with the deadlights up."

"Were you scared?"

"Scared to death. Especially when the ship stood right on end, and the water leaked under the cabin door. But now I wouldn't have missed it for anything. 'Twas the most exciting thing I ever knew."

His face lighted with admiration, but all for the ship. "She's a stout one, the *Dolphin*," he said. "She's come through many a worse blow than that." His eyes dwelt fondly on the topsails.

The passenger liner QE2 is longer than three football fields.

NOW

"What is happening?" Kit asked, noting the sudden activity along the deck. Four husky sailors in blue jackets and bright kerchiefs had hurried forward to man the capstan bars. Captain Eaton, in his good blue coat, was shouting orders from the quarterdeck. "Are we stopping here?"

"There are passengers to go ashore," Nat explained. "And we need food and water for the trip upriver. But we've missed the tide, and the wind is blowing too hard from the west for us to make the landing. We're going to anchor out here and take the longboat in to shore. That means I'd better look to the oars." He swung away, moving lightly and confidently; there was a bounce in his step that matched the laughter in his eyes.

With dismay, Kit saw the captain's wife among the passengers preparing to disembark. Must she say good-bye so soon to Mistress Eaton? They had shared the bond of being the only two women aboard the *Dolphin* and the older woman had been sociable and kindly. Now, catching Kit's eye, she came hurrying along the deck.

"Are you leaving the ship, Mistress Eaton?" Kit greeted her wistfully.

"Aye, didn't I tell you I'd be leaving you at Saybrook? But don't look so sad, child. 'Tis not far to Wethersfield, and we'll be meeting again."

"But I thought the *Dolphin* was your home!"

"In the wintertime it is, when we sail to the West Indies. But I was born in Saybrook, and in the spring I get to hankering for my house and garden. Besides, I'd never let on to my husband, but the summer trips are tedious, just back and forth up and down the river. I stay at home and tend my vegetables and my spinning like a proper housewife. Then, come November, when he sails for Barbados again, I'm ready enough to go with him. 'Tis a good life, and one of the best things about it is coming home in the springtime."

Kit glanced again at the forbidding shore. She could see nothing about it to put such a twinkle of anticipation in anyone's eye. Could there be some charm that was not visible from out here in the harbor? She spoke on a sudden impulse.

"Would there be room in the boat for me to ride to shore with you?" she begged. "I know it's silly, but there is America so close to me for the first time in my life—I can't bear not to set my foot upon it!"

"What a child you are, Kit," smiled Mrs. Eaton. "Sometimes 'tis hard to believe you are sixteen." She appealed to her husband. The captain scowled at the girl's wind-reddened cheeks and shining eyes, and then shrugged consent. As Kit gathered her heavy skirts about her and clambered down the swaying rope ladder, the men in the longboat good-naturedly shoved their bundles closer to make room for her. Her spirits bobbed like the whitecaps in the harbor as the boat pulled away from the black hull of the *Dolphin.*

As the prow scraped the landing piles, Nat leaped ashore and caught the hawser. He reached to help his mother, then stretched a sure hand to swing Kit over the boat's edge.

With a bound she was over the side and had set foot on America. She stood taking deep breaths of the salt, fish-tainted air, and looked about for someone to share her excitement. She was quite forgotten. A throng of men and boys on the wharf had noisily closed in on the three Eatons, and she could hear a busy catching up of the past months' news. The other passengers had hurried along the wharf to the dirt road beyond. Only three shabbily-dressed women lingered near her, and because she could not contain her eagerness, Kit smiled and would have spoken, but she was abruptly repulsed by their sharply curious eyes. One hand moved guiltily to her tangled brown curls. She must look a sight! No gloves, no cover for her hair, and her face rough and red from weeks of salt wind. But how ill-mannered of them to stare so! She pulled up the hood of her scarlet cloak and turned away. Embarrassment was a new sensation for Kit. No one on the island had ever presumed to stare like that at Sir Francis Tyler's granddaughter.

To make matters worse, America was behaving strangely underfoot. As she stepped forward, the wharf tilted upward, and she felt curiously lightheaded. Just in time a hand grasped her elbow.

"Steady there!" a voice warned. "You haven't got your land legs yet." Nat's blue eyes laughed down at her.

"It will wear off in a short time," his mother assured her. "Katherine, dear, I do hate to let you go on alone. You're sure your aunt will be waiting for you at Wethersfield? They say there's a Goodwife Cruff going aboard, and I'll tell her to keep an eye on you." With a quick clasp of Kit's hand she was gone and Nat, shouldering her trunk in one easy motion, followed her along the narrow dirt road. Which one of those queer little boxlike houses did they call home? Kit wondered.

She turned to watch the sailors stowing provisions into the longboat. She already regretted this impulsive trip ashore. There was no welcome for her at this chill Saybrook landing. She was grateful when at last the captain assembled the return group and she could climb back into the long-boat. Four new passengers were embark-ing for the trip up the river, a shabby, dour-looking man and wife and their scrawny little girl clutching a wooden toy, and a tall, angular young man with a pale narrow face and shoulder-length fair hair under a wide-brimmed black hat. Captain Eaton took his place aft without attempting any introduction. The men readied their oars. Then Nathaniel, coming back down the road on a run, slipped the rope from the mooring and as they pulled away from the wharf leaped nimbly to his place with the crew.

THEN
In 1569, Mercator published the first flat map of the world.

They were halfway across the harbor when a wail of anguish broke from the child. Before anyone could stop her the little girl had flung herself to her knees and teetered dangerously over the edge of the boat. Her mother leaned forward, grasped the woolen jumper and jerked her back, smacking her down with a sharp cuff.

"Ma! The dolly's gone!" the child wailed. "The dolly Grandpa made for me!"

Kit could see the little wooden doll, its arms sticking stiffly into the air, bobbing helplessly in the water a few feet away.

"Shame on you!" the woman scolded. "After the work he went to. All that fuss for a toy, and then the minute you get one you throw it away!"

"I was holding her up to see the ship! Please get her back, Ma! Please! I'll never drop it again!"

The toy was drifting farther and farther from the boat, like a useless twig in the current. No one in the boat made a move, or paid the slightest attention. Kit could not keep silent.

"Turn back, Captain," she ordered impulsively. " 'Twill be an easy thing to catch."

The captain did not even glance in her direction. Kit was not used to being ignored, and her temper flared. When a thin whimper from the child was silenced by a vicious cuff, her anger boiled over. Without a second's deliberation she acted. Kicking off her buckled shoes and dropping the woolen cloak, she plunged headlong over the side of the boat.

The shock of cold, totally unexpected, almost knocked her senseless. As her head came to the surface she could not catch her breath at all. But after a dazed second she sighted the bobbing piece of wood and instinctively struck out after it in vigorous strokes that set her blood moving again. She had the doll in her hand before her numbed mind realized that there had been a second splash, and as she turned back she saw that Nathaniel was in the water beside her, thrashing with a clumsy paddling motion. She could not help laughing as she passed him, and with a feeling of tri-

Cartographers at computers with high-resolution monitors produce up-to-the minute maps.

NOW

umph she beat him to the boat. The captain leaned to
drag her back over the side, and Nathaniel scrambled
in behind her without any assistance.

"Such water!" she gasped. "I never dreamed water
could be so cold!"

She shook back her wet hair, her cheeks glowing.
But her laughter died away at sight of all their faces.
Shock and horror and unmistakable anger stared
back at her. Even Nathaniel's young face was dark
with rage.

"You must be daft," the woman hissed. "To jump
into the river and ruin those clothes!"

Kit tossed her head. "Bother the clothes! They'll
dry. Besides, I have plenty of others."

"Then you might have a thought for somebody
else!" snapped Nat, slapping the water out of his drip-

ping breeches. "These are the only clothes I have."

Kit's eyes flashed. "Why did you jump in anyway? You needn't have bothered."

"You can be sure I wouldn't have," he retorted, "had I any idea you could swim."

Her eyes widened. "Swim?" she echoed scornfully. "Why my grandfather taught me to swim as soon as I could walk."

The others stared at her in suspicion. As though she had sprouted a tail and fins right before their eyes. What was the matter with these people? Not another word was uttered as the men pulled harder on their oars. A solid cloud of disapproval settled over the dripping girl, more chilling than the April breeze. Her high spirits plunged. She had made herself ridiculous. How many times had her grandfather cautioned her to think before she flew off the handle? She drew her knees and elbows tight under the red cloak and clenched her teeth to keep them from chattering. Water dripped off her matted hair and ran in icy trickles down her neck. Then, glancing defiantly from one hostile face to another, Kit found a small measure of comfort. The young man in the black hat was looking at her gravely, and all at once his lips twisted in spite of himself. A smile filled his eyes with such warmth and sympathy that a lump rose in Kit's throat, and she glanced away. Then she saw that the child, silently clutching her sodden doll, was staring at her with a gaze of pure worship.

Two hours later, dressed in a fresh green silk, Kit was spreading the wet dress and the woolen cloak to dry on the sun-warmed planking of the deck when her glance was caught by the wide black hat, and she looked up to see the new passenger coming toward her.

"If you will give me leave," he said, with stiff courtesy, removing the hat to reveal a high fine forehead, "I would like to introduce myself. I am John Holbrook, bound for Wethersfield, which I learn is your destination as well."

Kit had not forgotten that comforting smile. "I am Katherine Tyler," she answered forthrightly. "I am on the way to Wethersfield to live with my aunt, Mistress Wood."

"Is Matthew Wood your uncle then? His name is well known along the river."

"Yes, but I have never seen him, nor my aunt either. I do not even know very much about her, just that she was my mother's sister back in England, and that she was very beautiful."

The young man looked puzzled. "I have never met your aunt," he said politely. "I came to look for you now because I felt I should ask your pardon for the way we all behaved toward you this morning. After all, it was only a kind thing you meant to do, to get the toy back for the child."

" 'Twas a very foolish thing, I realize now," she admitted. "I am forever doing foolish things. Even so, I can't understand why it should make everyone so angry."

He considered this gravely. "You took us aback, that is all. We were all sure you would drown before our eyes. It was astonishing to see you swimming."

"But can't you swim?"

He flushed. "I cannot swim a stroke, nor could anyone else on this ship, I warrant, except Nat who was born on the water. Where in England could they have taught you a thing like that?"

"Not England. I was born on Barbados."

"Barbados!" He stared. "The heathen island in the West Indies?"

" 'Tis no heathen island. 'Tis as civilized as England, with a famous town and fine streets and shops. My grandfather was one of the first plantation owners, with a grant from the King."

"You are not a Puritan then?"

"Puritan? You mean a Roundhead? One of those traitors who murdered King Charles?"

A spark of protest flashed across his mild gray eyes. He started to speak, then thought better of it, and asked gently, "You are going to stay here in Connecticut?"

Under his serious gaze Kit was suddenly uneasy. She had had enough questioning. "Do you live in Wethersfield yourself?" she turned the tables. The young man shook his head.

"My home is in Saybrook, but I am going to Wethersfield to study under the Reverend Bulkeley. In another year I hope to be ready to take a church of my own."

A clergyman! She might have guessed it. His very smile had a touch of solemnness. But even as she thought it, she was surprised by the humor that quirked his fine straight lips.

"I mistrust you will be a surprise to the good people of Wethersfield," he said mildly. "What will they make of you, I wonder?"

Kit started. Had he guessed? There was no one who could possibly have told him. She had kept her secret even from the captain's wife. Before she could ask what he meant, she was diverted by the sight of Nat Eaton swinging along the deck in their direction. His thin clothing had dried on him, but the friendly grin of that morning had been replaced by an aloof and mocking smile that showed only too well that his morning's ducking had not been forgotten.

"My father sent me to find you, Mistress Tyler." One couldn't have guessed, by his tone, that he had ever addressed her before. "Since my mother has left the ship he thinks it best that you eat at board with Goodwife Cruff and her family."

Kit wrinkled up her nose. "Ugh," she exclaimed, "that sour face of hers will curdle my food."

Nat laughed shortly. " 'Tis certain she expects you will curdle hers," he answered. "She has been insisting to my father that you are a witch. She says no respectable woman could keep afloat in the water like that."

"How dare she!" Kit flared, indignant as much at his tone as at the dread word he uttered so carelessly.

"Don't you know about the water trial?" Nat's eyes deliberately taunted her. " 'Tis a sure test. I've seen it myself. A true witch will always float. The innocent ones just sink like a stone."

He was obviously paying her back for the morning's humiliation. But she was surprised to see that John Holbrook was not at all amused. His solemn young face was even more grave than before.

"That is not a thing to be laughed at," he said. "Is the woman serious, Nat?"

Nat shrugged. "She'd worked up quite a gale," he admitted. "But my father has smoothed her down. He knows Barbados. He explained that the sea is always warm and that even respectable people sometimes swim in it. All the same, Mistress Katherine," he added, with a quizzical look, "now that you're in Connecticut I'd advise you to forget that you ever learned."

"No danger," Kit shuddered. "I wouldn't go near your freezing river again for the world."

She had made them both laugh, but underneath her nonchalance, Kit felt uneasy. In spite of his mocking tone, Nat had unmistakably warned her, just as she knew now that John Holbrook had been about to warn her. There was something strange about this country of America, something that they all seemed to share and understand and she did not. She was only partially reassured when John said, with another of those surprising flashes of gentle humor, "I shall sit with you at supper, if I may. Just to make sure that no one's food gets curdled."

Research Spelled Fun

Elizabeth George Speare

If I could come into your classroom and visit with you, I know that one of the first questions you would ask me is one I have been asked many times—how did you get the idea for this book? That is a very hard question to answer. Ideas come unexpectedly, out of the blue, and they are usually tiny and elusive, just a hint of something tantalizing that may vanish altogether but may just possibly grow into a real story. Sometimes the idea comes from a vivid memory, or from an incident in a history book, or perhaps just from a glimpse of a strange face. Surprisingly, however, I can tell you about the idea that grew into the story of *The Witch of Blackbird Pond.*

I was living in Wethersfield, Connecticut, a very old town on the Connecticut River, first settled in 1634, with a fascinating history I wanted to write about. One day, when my husband and I were walking along the meadows that border the river, I saw in my imagination a girl walking there, and somehow she seemed to me lonely and unhappy. I did not see her clearly, but that quick glimpse stayed in my mind. I wanted to know why she was lonely and unhappy, and sometime later I stumbled upon the answer. In an old book about colonial America I came upon the story of a little girl who lived on the sunny island of Barbados and who was sent, like many English children of that day, to be educated in Boston. In her grandmother's strait-laced New England home, this little girl was cold and miserable. Suddenly I saw again my imaginary girl, not a child, living in the bleak Puritan town of Wethersfield so different from her home in Barbados. Of course she was unhappy! From that tiny spark the story of Kit Tyler began to grow.

As I thought about this girl and pictured her arrival in New England, other characters came to join her—two young men and a child with disagreeable parents. Somehow they would play their parts in the story to come, though I did not know just how.

Of course all this time that I was dreaming about my imaginary characters I was also doing what people call RESEARCH, which for me is spelled FUN. I love to poke about in dusty corners of libraries, finding bits and pieces of history, which give me the feel and taste and smell of bygone days. I want to know how my characters lived, what they ate, what they wore, what they thought about and what events were taking place in the world around them.

So bit by bit, over a year and a half, a whole new world grew in my mind and the ancient house and town became as real to me as the room where I sat with my typewriter. It was like living two lives. Every day I could step into that other world and learn with Kit to spin yarn, to stir a kettle over an open fire, to sit all day long on a hard bench on the Sabbath. And I watched my characters grow and change and work out their lives in ways I never imagined when I first saw that lonely girl in the meadows. I hope that the story will carry to my readers some of the excitement I felt as I watched them grow.

THINKING ABOUT IT

1 When you read about Kit Tyler, you are looking back over 300 years. Is Kit so different from people you've known? Is she different from the people around her? Is she headed for trouble?

2 How does the author keep the action moving along while still taking time to give you historical details of time and place? Find a good example in "First Glimpse of America" and explain how she combines plot with details of setting.

3 Obviously, Kit faces some problems. Think what those problems are or might be. What advice can you give to help her?

Historical
FICTION
an Opportunity and Challenge

By Violet Harris

What is Africa to me:
Copper sun or scarlet sea,
Jungle star or jungle track,
Strong bronzed men, or regal black....
  from "Heritage" by Countee Cullen, 1925

What images do you have of Africa, and what do you know about the great nation-states and rulers in African history? Since not much was put down in writing until recently, you may not be familiar with the fascinating events in Africa's history. Research done throughout the world in the twentieth century has resulted in books and documents that tell this history. The scholarly works could provide writers of historical fiction with a wealth of facts about people and places.

Who were some of the great leaders in African history? Have you heard of Sundiata, an early ruler of the

Opposite page: Benin Ivory Mask (Nigeria)

empire of Mali? According to legend, he was the only one of eleven brothers, heirs to the throne of Kangaba, not assassinated by the cruel tyrant Sumanguru. Was he spared because he had been born with weak legs and couldn't walk as a child? Or was it because he followed a warning and went into exile until he had grown strong enough to challenge the tyrant? You could write a fascinating story about Sundiata—the lion king—and how he gathered a great army to defeat Sumanguru.

Another colorful leader was Mansa Musa, the grandson of one of Sundiata's sisters. Imagine how the citizens of Mali felt when he made his famous pilgrimage to Mecca using scores of camels laden with gold and other items!

The valiant war efforts of Queen Nzingha, who led a fierce army of women against the Portuguese in the sixteenth century, would provide material for an exciting story.

What about the warrior Idris Alooma? The story of how he created an army of soldiers and outfitted them in iron helmets and chain mail similar to that worn by the knights of Europe could be the background for an exciting adventure story.

In the latter part of the seventeenth century, Osei Tutu brought together the great chiefs of the Ashanti nation. Legend says that the chiefs proclaimed Osei Tutu king of the new Ashanti nation after a golden stool descended from heaven as he was explaining his plan. A story could be told about his efforts to organize government, establish a constitution, and create a national festival.

What are the important places in African history? Certainly they include the nation-state Mali, which was an undisputed center of power for several hundred years after its beginnings in the thirteenth century. Cities such as Timbuktu and Jenne that were involved in the gold trade became centers of scholarship as well as commerce.

Historical fiction, with its combination of fact, legend, and imagination, can portray a different time period in an interesting way and help the reader experience the past. *The Legend of Tarik* by Walter Dean Myers is one recent historical fiction/fantasy that captures some of the grandeur and tumult of Medieval North Africa. As a boy, Tarik witnessed the killing of his family by the legions of El Muerte, an evil warrior. After being rescued by two wise old men, Tarik set out on a quest to end the cruelty of El Muerte.

Because not much was known about the history of Africa until recently, *The Legend of Tarik* is one of only a few books of historical fiction about Africa. Today there is opportunity and challenge to create historical fiction about Africa. If you study the fascinating people and events in African history, *you* might portray them in a work of historical fiction.

PORTRAIT OF
JUAN DE PAREJA

BY DIEGO RODRÍGUEZ DE SILVA Y VELÁZQUEZ

I
Am Set
FREE

By Elizabeth Borton de Treviño

*This story is told by Juan de Pareja, slave to the
great seventeenth-century Spanish painter
Velázquez, who painted portraits of King Philip IV
and his court. At that time, it was forbidden by law
for slaves to learn or practice the arts.*

The King was in the habit of coming often, at odd
hours, to pass a short while in the studio.

"You have only to see me as your sovereign when
I speak," he told Master. "I wish to be able to slip in
and out, quietly, without any formality, to sit and
enjoy a painting of my choosing, and feel at peace."
He had given me orders that I was not to "see" him
either unless he spoke, whenever he came unaccompa-
nied. "I wish to spend a little time in complete
invisibility," he told us, smiling.

So cakes and wine were always waiting for him in the studio, and one of his own easy chairs. His accustomed hour to drop in was late afternoon, before he had to dress for some court function.

Long ago I had heard some of the courtiers in Rubens's* train say that the Spanish court was the stiffest and most boring in Europe. I am sure His Majesty found it so, but did not know what to do about it.

So he escaped, and sat sipping his wine, and gazing at some picture of Master's, which he had turned round from where they were stacked, and set up, at some distance from his chair.

I had secretly painted a large canvas, for Master was frequently in attendance on Mistress in her bedroom, where she rested many hours, and to which she called him to chat with her. She often felt lonely and needed him near.

My subject was the King's favorite hounds. All were dead, and they had not been contemporaries, but they had been favorites of his, and I knew that he would recognize them.

The three hounds (one of them was Corso) lay in a forest glade; a shaft of golden light came through the branches of the trees and lay warmly on them. One dog was turned toward me, tongue drooping from his mouth, the black doggy lips turned up in a smile; one looked away into the distance with pricked ears; and one dozed, nose on paws. I had taken their likenesses carefully from many paintings of Master, and I had worked out the setting with all the art of which I was capable.

Having received Communion and commended myself to Our Lady, I took that canvas and put it amongst those of Master turned against the wall, to await the King's pleasure. Then, trembling and already

*Rubens, a famous painter who lived from 1577–1640.

D·112

frightened, I awaited the hour when I would have to confess.

Several days went by. His Majesty was indisposed and remained in his apartments.

Master was painting another mirror arrangement, fussily moving his mirrors about, checking lights and reflections; he paid no attention to me and did not notice that I was nervous.

Then my hour struck.

It was late in the afternoon. Master was not painting, but sitting at his desk making out some accounts and writing to order special pigments from Flanders. The door of the studio opened quietly and His Majesty stepped in, looking around in his uncertain, apologetic way. He was dressed for some court ceremony: black velvet shoes and long black silk stockings, black velvet trousers, but instead of a doublet he wore only a white shirt of thin cotton, and a dressing gown of dark silk brocade. I supposed that after contemplating a picture he meant to return to his rooms, put on his doublet, call the barber to shave him and curl his hair and mustache, and then attach his big white starched ruff at the last moment.

He pulled out his chair, sat, and stretched his long legs with a deep sigh. He smiled amiably at Master, who smiled back warmly, affectionately, and then went on with his accounts.

After a short time the King rose and went toward the wall. He stood hesitating a moment, and then turned a canvas toward him. It was mine. In the late light, the faithful hounds shone out from the dark background, sunlight on their glistening hides, light in their big, loving, dark eyes. His Majesty stood transfixed; he had never seen that canvas before. I could watch his always-slow mind adjusting to the fact that this was a portrait of his own favorite hounds.

I threw myself on my knees before him.

"I beg mercy, Sire," I pleaded. "The painting is mine. I have been working secretly all these years, with bits of canvas and color, copying the works of Master, to learn from them, and trying some original subjects by myself. I know very well that this is against the law. Master has never even suspected and has had nothing to do with my treachery. I am willing to endure whatever punishment you mete out to me."

I remained on my knees, begging the Virgin to remember my promise, praying and asking her forgiveness and her help. Opening my eyes, I saw the feet of His Majesty moving nervously about. Evidently he did not know what to reply. Then he cleared his throat and took a deep breath. The feet in the velvet shoes remained quiet.

"What... what shall we do... with this... this ... disobedient slave?" I heard his voice lisping and stuttering, as he turned toward Master.

Still on my knees, I saw Master's neat small feet, in their shoes of Cordovan leather, approach and place themselves in front of my picture. He studied it some time in silence, and the King waited.

Then Master spoke. "Have I your Majesty's leave to write an urgent letter before I answer?"

"You have it."

Master returned to his desk and I heard his quill scratching against the paper. His Majesty returned to his chair and threw himself into it. I remained where I was, praying with all my might.

Master rose, and his feet moved toward me.

"Get up, Juan," he said. He put a hand under my elbow and helped me to my feet. He was looking at me with the gentle affection he had always shown me.

Las Meninas

By Diego Rodríguez de Silva y Velázquez

He took my hand and put a letter into it. I have worn that letter sewed into a silk envelope and pinned inside my shirt ever since. The letter said:

To Whom It May Concern
I have this day given freedom to my slave Juan de Pareja, who shall have all the rights and honors of a free man, and further, I hereby name him my Assistant, with the duties and salary thereto pertaining.

Diego Rodríguez de Silva y Velázquez

Master took the letter gently from my hand, after I had read it, and took it to the King who, reading, smiled radiantly. It was the first time in all those years that I had seen His Majesty smile. His teeth were small and uneven, but that smile seemed to me as beautiful as any I had ever seen.

The letter was given back to me, and I stood there, tears of joy streaming from my eyes.

"You were saying, Sire, something about a slave?" inquired Master softly. "I have no slave."

I seized his hand, to carry it to my lips.

"No, no," cried Master, snatching his hand back. "You owe me no gratitude, my good friend. The contrary. I am ashamed that in my selfish preoccupations I did not long ago give you what you have earned so well and what I know you will grace with your many virtues. You are to be my assistant if you wish, as you are my friend always."

"I am pleased," said His Majesty, and rose to his feet. At the door, before he left, he turned and said again, "I am pleased."

We waited, Master and I, side by side, bowing, as the King sailed down the corridor, his dressing gown billowing out behind him.

"Let us pack up our things, Juan (he never again

called me Juanico), and go home. Mistress is fretful when I am not more often at her side. And I am tired."

"As your assistant, Master..."

"Now do not call me Master any more. Call me Diego."

"I cannot. You are still Master. My Master, as you were Master to the apprentices, and to other painters. Master means teacher, does it not?"

"Yes."

"I was never ashamed to call you my Master, and I am not ashamed now. I shall always give you the respect of that title."

"As you wish."

We were walking through the streets of Madrid toward our home. I took each step with a new spring in my knees, a new joy in my heart, for I walked as a free man, beside my Teacher.

"But, Master," I said, as we crossed the Plaza Mayor, "you were in error when you said that you had no slave. There is Lolis."

"Lolis belongs to my wife," he told me.

I determined to make this a day radiant in my memory in every way.

"Master, when we were in Italy, you told me that I could ask anything of this hand" (and I took his right hand lightly in my own) "and you would give it me. Now I know what to ask for."

He stopped in the square where the last rays of the sun struck level against us. "You want Lolis," he said, smiling.

"I wish to marry her. If she will have me."

"I will speak to my wife about it. I see no reason why you should not marry if you both wish it," he answered, and we continued to stroll in silence.

Inside our house—that house where I had lived so many years in peace of mind and spirit, even though I had not been free—everything now seemed new to me. The corridors, so much a part of my daily existence, the dark heavy carved furniture, the life-sized crucifix with its small glow and flicker of light always in a glass bowl at the feet of the Christ, the dark red velvet curtains now drawn against the declining day to keep out the humors and evils of night—all were dear and known to me, but somehow fresh and new.

We had no sooner entered than Lolis came running toward us, finger to lip.

"The Mistress has been in much pain today," she whispered, "and I have just now been able to get her to sleep."

"I will not go up then," answered Master. "Bring us some wine, please, Lolis, and some walnuts."

We went into the dining room. Very often Paquita came, with her two little children, but today the house was quiet and still. We ate our nuts and drank wine together. I could see that Master was worried, and I knew why. Mistress was more and more often ill and weak, and sometimes she lay and cried.

THEN
It took Michelangelo four years to complete the Sistine Chapel painting he began in 1508.

When I went into the kitchen later Lolis came and laid her head on my shoulder. She was not weeping— I have always been quick to tears, but I have never seen one glittering on her lashes—but she sighed deeply.

"My poor lady," she grieved. "I have come to be fond of her, Juan. And soon we will have to give her some opium to stop the awful paroxysms of coughing. The King could get it for Master. It will be a sad time now, Juan, until God calls her."

Actually, as sometimes happens, Mistress rallied and seemed much better a few days later. She got up and was dressed and began to eat some of the dainties Lolis had prepared for her. On the second evening she came to the supper table and smiled and seemed very happy, sitting at Master's side. She ate quite a bit of supper and did not cough once.

Master looked up at me suddenly and I could read his intention in his eyes. Turning to her, he said, "*Mi vida*, I have given our good friend Juan his freedom and he is now my honored assistant. He will take many duties off my shoulders and I will rest more and be more often with you. I know you have been lonely with our daughter married and gone from the house."

"Ah yes!" cried Mistress, her thin face lighting up. "That is why I have been ailing. I have been lonely."

"And Juan wishes to marry. He has given his heart to you, Lolis. What do you say?"

Mistress clasped her hands. "Lolis!" she cried. "What is your answer?"

I remember that Lolis was wearing a dress of pale almond green, and she had bound back her hair with a rose-colored scarf.

"I can answer as I wish?" asked Lolis.

"Of course."

"My answer is No."

I felt as if my heart had been pierced with a dagger. Lolis saw the hurt in my face.

"It is not that I do not like him," she said, in her deep soft voice. "He is a good kind man, but I do not wish to bear any children into slavery."

Master's quiet voice was heard. "You are right, Lolis. Juan is now a free man. And I am sure my wife would like to give you your freedom, as a wedding gift. Isn't it so, my love?"

Mistress took her cue and answered at once, for she was always eager to please Master in every way she knew, and now that she was ill, more than ever, it seemed.

THE WATER-SELLER OF SEVILLE

BY DIEGO RODRÍGUEZ DE SILVA Y VELÁZQUEZ

"It is so indeed. If you will hand me the paper and pen and inkpot, I will write the letter of manumission now."

Mistress wrote the letter and put it into Lolis's hand.

"My dear Lolis," she said, "you are as free now, as you have always been in your spirit, I think. But I would ask a favor of you. Please stay on as my nurse. Do not leave me . . . just yet."

Lolis put the letter in her bosom, and she looked with tenderness at Mistress.

"I am glad to be free," she said. "More than you can know. I never dreamed that it would come to pass so soon, though I had seen in the future that it would be so, one day. Just as I have seen that I would marry Juan. Yes, I shall stay with you, Mistress, as long as you want me. And I thank you."

Quietly she gathered up some dishes and left the room softly.

Master gave me permission with his eyes, and I followed Lolis out into the kitchen. She was in a corner, on her knees, praying.

"I was thanking God," she told me. "I have prayed for this every day of my life."

"And you will marry me, Lolis?"

"Yes. But you could have found a better woman, Juan. I am proud and haughty and sometimes I have a sharp tongue."

"It is you I want, just as you are."

She came into my arms then, and let me caress her hair, her cheek and her forehead.

"I have resented being a slave," she said. "I could not feel grateful in my heart, for deep inside me I resented being bound. I know that God made us all free and that no man should own another. I hated serving people because I was a slave and had to do their will. Only here in this house I had some peace because you are all kind and Mistress is sweet and affectionate. I will do my best to make her last days comfortable. But I am not like you, Juan, grateful and loving. I *hated* being owned! It was all I could do, some days, to keep the hot words inside my mouth and the resentment out of my voice."

"Never mind. Everything is different now. And if we have children, they will be born free."

"Yes. But many of our race are not, Juan. My heart aches for them."

"Some day," I assured her, "some day, I know that all men will be free."

"It will take a long time, and much bloodshed, before that day comes," said Lolis, somberly.

THINKING ABOUT IT

1 There really was such a painter, such a king, and such a man as Juan de Pareja. In this historical fiction, you see and hear them. You learn their worries. You experience their warmth to each other. What do you think about them? What do you wonder?

2 The five characters seem to need each other. How has this author shown this need? Read examples to show it.

3 Another way to know the past, besides reading historical fiction, is to look at its art. Find a picture of a sculpture, painting, or other piece of art from Spain or Africa. What does the art tell you about the artist and the time in which the artist lived?

History

Langston Hughes

The past has been a mint
Of blood and sorrow.
That must not be
True of tomorrow.

In the Museum

Charlotte Zolotow

The horse from 200 B.C.
is made of stone,
but the way he holds his head
shows
someone long ago
loved a horse like him,
though now
both horse and sculptor
                      are dead.

What a Precious
GIFT, LIFE

By Erik Christian Haugaard

My fifteenth summer was as free of troubles as the spring sky is of clouds. Two weeks after my arrival in Iida Castle a messenger came from Kofuchu bearing a dispatch from Lord Takeda. The messenger was not one of the usual young soldiers but a high-ranking samurai who had traveled with ten mounted retainers. He was alone with Lord Akiyama for several hours; we never found out what they had discussed, for the doors and screens were kept firmly closed. The next day Lord Akiyama announced that he would leave for Tsutsujigasaki Castle in a few days' time, taking most of the soldiers and samurai with him.

Only a small garrison was to be left at Iida Castle under the command of an old samurai whom we youngsters had dubbed "Lord Inago" because of the way he walked. One of his legs was stiff from an old wound, which gave him a jumping gait like a grasshopper's. For two days I was kept in suspense, not knowing if I was to go or to stay at the castle. When I finally learned that the youngest among the messengers were to remain, I was bitterly disappointed. Fate had cheated me of an opportunity to show my worth on the battlefield.

Lord Akiyama left at the head of his army on a beautiful day; the sun shone from a clear sky and made armor and banners appear doubly bright and colorful. By this time we all knew that Lord Takeda was planning to invade the province of Suruga as soon as the rice harvest was over. As I watched some of the older messengers ride by, I felt so angry that I was near to tears. Suddenly I felt a hand on my shoulder, and I looked around and saw Yoshitoki.

"Some of them will come back heroes," he said, "but there are others who will not come back at all. The heroes will be given land and some of the spoil of battle by Lord Takeda. The others, those who won't come back," Yoshitoki lowered his voice to a whisper, "they will be given land, too, but not so much— just enough for a grave."

THEN
Samurai of the sixteenth century used curved swords for protection and for battle.

Naturally I knew that people died in battle, that the ground was sometimes covered in corpses after the fighting had ceased. Although I had heard of rivers that turned red with the blood of the dying, I had never imagined myself among them. I nodded soberly as if those very words he had spoken expressed my feelings too. Yoshitoki smiled; I am sure that he knew what I had been thinking.

"We are lucky," he said. "We shall have the castle almost to ourselves. The Grasshopper is easy-going and will not need us much; we will be free to hunt and fish. . . . I am now the oldest of the messengers."

All of a sudden I realized that the two messengers whom I liked least were to accompany Lord Akiyama. It was true what Yoshitoki had said: we would be free to hunt and fish. Lord Inago would not be a hard master, that was certain. As the last of the soldiers passed by, I turned to Yoshitoki.

"I was angry because I was left behind," I confessed. "I wanted to be among the soldiers whom Lord Akiyama took along. I was very foolish."

"No!" Yoshitoki shook his head. "I think you are destined to live and I to die. That is why you are eager to prove yourself in battle and I am pleased to have yet another year to live." He grinned and stretched himself.

For several months Yoshitoki and I explored every path and valley within a day's ride of the castle. We tracked the deer and the wild boar and surprised a wolf in her lair. Armed with bows and arrows, we killed many a rabbit and brought back enough game to please Lord Inago and make him only too willing to let us hunt for more. We were up so early that we often saw the fox returning from the nightly hunt; we rose with the sun and, tired as a couple of bear cubs that have played all day, we fell asleep as it set.

Yet while we strutted the earth like immortals, the warmth of the friendship between Yoshitoki and me was so intense that the memory of it can even now warm the body of a frail old man. We were like two small clouds drifting in an endless sky.

Few duties kept us away from our pleasures, but at the end of the tenth month we were given an assignment. We were to carry a message to Kofuchu, to Tsutsujigasaki Castle. The best of the horses had gone with Lord Akiyama, but we were allowed to take our pick of the remainder. I was immensely pleased when we were given weapons, only a sword each, and again not of the best quality, but the same as the foot soldiers carried. We were also given a purse for the expenses during the journey and papers to prove that

Modern weaponry includes launchers with missiles that can intercept enemy aircraft and missiles.

NOW

we were traveling on an errand for Lord Takeda, so that we did not have to pay toll at the gates on the road. We felt immensely important the morning we started out. Yoshitoki's horse was saddled, but I rode bareback as there was no saddle left in a condition to be used.

The first day passed uneventfully. We followed the road that runs along the bottom of the valley near the river; this is a well-traveled road with plenty of inns in the villages where food may be obtained. We felt very grand as we sat eating our meals and, like young lords, ordered the servant girl to bring more tea or another dish of rice.

On the second day we reached Takato Castle; here, too, the garrison was small and consisted of the very young and very oldest soldiers. They told us that Lord Shingen had been victorious and that the army was expected to return within a month. Lord Katsuyori, the governor of the castle, was not there but was with his father. As at Iida, an old and trusted samurai had been left in charge.

The following morning, just as we were leaving, two Buddhist monks appeared and asked permission to travel in our company. They were on foot but had an old horse carrying sutras that they were taking to a monastery in Kai. Though not pleased, we were flattered and tried to make excuses; the monks insisted that they would like our company for safety as we traveled through the mountains. They claimed to be followers of the sect of Nichiren traveling to the main temple of their sect, Kuon-ji. It is a sect of Buddhism I do not care much for; its adherents are strong-willed and quarrelsome. What is pleasant and agreeable in this world they regard as sinful; they are quick to attack others for their vanity, but I have always found them the vainest themselves. In his book of advice, the great general, Lord Kansuke, warns against quarrelsome traveling companions, but there was no getting rid of them so we set out just after sunrise.

The monks walked quickly and had little trouble keeping up with us; their bodies were thin and muscular, as if they were used to traveling. They were well past their youth, though still in the prime of their strength, and I could not help feeling that it was not long since their heads had been shaven for the first time. I felt sure that they had been samurai, guessing this from the look of contempt the younger of them had given my sword, as if he had been used to better. They say that the blade of the sword is a mirror that reflects its owner's soul; if that is true, then mine was a sorry one.

Midmorning we rested by a small brook, first drinking from its clear water ourselves and then letting our horses quench their thirst. The two monks asked a lot of questions but answered few themselves. It struck me that there was not much point in carrying sutras to Kuon-ji; surely there were plenty of prayer rolls there already as the monks in the temple made them? I did not ask, for I suspected that our traveling companions were not monks but bandits. It was not so much our swords that they needed for protection, but our traveling permits. As couriers carrying a message from one castle to another we would be allowed through the toll-gates without much scrutiny and so would our traveling companions—our very presence would vouch for them. I glanced at Yoshitoki. The wary expression on his face convinced me that he had come to the same conclusion.

Just before noon we came to a path that led off to the right. We were now far into the mountains and one of the monks claimed that this was a short cut which would save us half a day's journey. The path was less traveled than the one we were on and looked best suited for some dark deed. I felt certain that should we enter it we would not return but would be left somewhere in the forest as food for foxes or wolves. I tried to ride ahead but the monks blocked the passage with their horse. My hand felt for the hilt of my sword, but before I had a chance to draw it our traveling companions drew two shiny and sharp-looking weapons from the pack on their horse.

"Young legs are best trained and grow strongest by walking!" said one of the monks with a grin while with his sword he indicated that we should dismount. I looked at Yoshitoki; he had drawn his sword and his horse was standing near the rump of the monks' nag. One of the monks was holding the reins, and the other was leaning against the flank of the animal. Suddenly Yoshitoki stuck his sword as hard as he could into the rump of their old nag. Whinnying loudly the horse jumped in pain, dragging one monk with her and throwing the other off balance. The road was free, so we dug our heels into the sides of our animals and galloped ahead.

We galloped until we thought ourselves safe, then reined in our horses and looked at each other.

"They were bandits!" we both exclaimed at the same moment and then started to laugh. This was high adventure, a story to tell on our return. Then I recalled that Lord Kansuke had also recommended that people who wanted to take short cuts should not be trusted. I told Yoshitoki this and he laughed, saying that the path we had not taken would surely have been a short cut to death.

There is nothing that can make a man feel more alive than to have been near death. Suddenly you realize what a precious gift your life is, and your eyes open to the beauty of the world around you. Such were our feelings as we traveled on. Once in a while we would glance at each other and then smile contentedly.

Pulling It All Together

1 Are the two young men foolish or brave? Will they still feel the same about going to battle, or has this incident changed them? Would they be good characters to get to know? What do you think of them?

2 In this book you've read of several places and times, and the authors have shown you several ways of writing about them—time-travel fantasy, historical fiction, drama, poetry, nonfiction. Now choose your own combination. What time and place, and what type of writing will you choose to read? Explain.

3 You could try trading time slots with any character in this book—well, at least for a day. What character will you trade with? What happens to you? What happens to him or her?

Another Book by Erik Christian Haugaard

British warships prepare a trap for John Paul Jones and his crew of rebels from the colonies in *A Boy's Will* by Erik Christian Haugaard.

Books to Enjoy

LEONARDO DA VINCI
by Ernest Raboff
Harper, 1987

Beautiful full-color reproductions of da Vinci's master-pieces illustrate this biography of the famous artist. The text is hand-lettered, and there are illustrations of his sketches, showing the stages of his work.

SWEETWATER
by Laurence Yep
Harper, 1973

Imagine a time slot a thousand years in the future! In this unusual science-fiction book, thirteen-year-old Tyree, a descendant of the first people from Earth to colonize the star Harmony, struggles with the hydras and seadragons invading his half-flooded city.

ISLAND OF THE OGRES
by Lensey Namioka
Harper, 1989

Kajiro is a *ronin*, a samurai without a master. But the vil-lagers mistake him for a famous warrior and expect him to save them from ogres. Kajiro soon discovers mysteries the terrified island people never imagined.

MY NAME IS NOT ANGELICA
by Scott O'Dell
Houghton, 1989

Raisha, a sixteen-year-old Senegalese girl, is betrayed and sold into slavery, along with Konje, a young king she plans to marry. The couple have different ways of pre-serving their love and dignity.

THE KNIGHT AND THE SQUIRE
by Argentina Palacios
Doubleday, 1979

Don Quixote makes absurd mistakes. That's a wayside inn, not a castle; and those are windmills, not long-armed giants. Read about the comic adventures of the dreamer-knight and his humorous, practical squire.

EXPLORATION AND DISCOVERY
by John Man
Gareth Stevens, 1990

Explorers have many motives—to trade, to steal, to learn, to become famous, to spread a religion. This book includes maps and pictures to help describe famous explorations throughout history.

EL GUERO
by Elizabeth Borton de Treviño
Farrar, Straus, Giroux, 1989

El Guero's family is exiled to the wild, bandit-infested frontier of Baja, California. When his father is jailed for trying to uphold the law, El Guero must travel through dangerous wilderness to get help.

THE SECOND MRS. GIACONDA
by E. L. Konigsburg
Atheneum, 1975

Famous people all over Italy beg Leonardo da Vinci to paint their portraits. Why does he paint the wife of an unimportant merchant instead? Salai, Leonardo's apprentice, tells how his master came to paint the *Mona Lisa*.

Literary Terms

Characterization   Characterization is the methods an author uses to acquaint you with a person. The author of "First Glimpse of America" introduces us to Kit Tyler by describing her appearance, her actions, and her words. Recall that she wears buckled shoes, a woolen cloak, and heavy skirts. When she jumps into the water to save the doll, we learn that she is impulsive and fearless. Her words show that she doesn't place importance on how she looks: "Bother the clothes. They'll dry."

Foreshadowing   Foreshadowing is a hint, or clue, about what will happen later in the story. When the samurai in "What a Precious Gift, Life" says that a great general, in his book of advice, warned against quarrelsome traveling companions, there is foreshadowing of what is to come.

Historical Fiction   Historical fiction is a made-up yet realistic story that takes place in the past. It is based on historical fact, and may include real historical figures as well as characters created by the author. The real Queen Elizabeth and the child Elizabeth, who is a fictional person, are both characters in "What Is This Place?"

Metaphor   A metaphor is a comparison between two things that are really quite different. When the child Elizabeth awakes in the pigpen in Iowa, she "struggles to keep her footing in a sea of pigs." The comparison of the pigpen to a sea helps you picture the scene in a new way.

Mood   Mood is the feeling, or atmosphere, in a story or poem. The mood of "Luther and Breck" is joyful. This mood is created by the picture of the two boys at play, pretending to be brave knights fighting dragons. The mood of "In the Museum" is one of wonder, created by the description of the stone sculpture of the horse.

Setting   The setting is the time and place of the events in a story. The setting may be integral to the plot, and this is especially true in historical fiction. In the opening paragraphs of "First Glimpse of America," the author describes the time, a morning in mid-April, 1687, and place, a ship on the Connecticut River. "What a Precious Gift, Life" could not take place anywhere except Japan during the period of the samurai.

Theme   Theme is the main idea that runs through a selection. Often the theme is not directly stated, but it is the understanding you get from all of the events that occur. In "I Am Set Free," Juan and Lolis are slaves who gain their freedom. The theme is that freedom is valued by people, and, in fact, one of the most important things in life.

Time-Travel Fantasy   A fantasy is a story that could not happen. In a time-travel fantasy, characters move from one time period into another with the help of a device an author invents. The characters may find themselves dressed in strange clothing and involved in situations they do not understand. Even the words they hear may be unfamiliar. "What Is This Place?" is an example of a time-travel fantasy.

Glossary

Vocabulary from your selections

ad her ent (ad hir′ənt), *n.* a faithful supporter or follower: *an adherent of the conservative party.*

af flic tion (ə flik′shən), *n.* **1** condition of continued pain or distress; misery. **2** cause of continued pain or distress; misfortune.

a gue (ā′gyü), *n.* **1** a malarial fever with chills and sweating that alternate at regular intervals. **2** any fit of shaking or shivering; chill.

a stray (ə strā′), *adj., adv.* **1** out of the right way; off. **2** in or into error.

bear ing (ber′ing, bar′ing), *n.* **1** way of standing, sitting, walking, or behaving; manner. **2** connection in thought or meaning; reference; relation: *Your question has no bearing on the problem.* **3 bearings,** *pl.* position in relation to other things; direction: *We had no compass, so we got our bearings from the stars.* **4** part of a machine on or in which a shaft, journal, pivot, pin, etc., turns or slides. A bearing serves to support the moving part and to reduce friction by turning with the motion. **5** act, power, or time of producing or bringing forth: *a tree past bearing.* **6** that which is produced; fruit; crop. **7** power of abiding; endurance.

bowl er (bō′lər), *n.* **1** person who bowls. **2** BRITISH. a derby hat.

brig an tine (brig′ən tēn′, brig′ən tīn), *n.* ship with two masts. The foremast is square-rigged; the mainmast is fore-and-aft-rigged.

Bud dha (bü′də, bùd′ə), *n.* 563?-483? B.C., a religious teacher of northern India and the founder of Buddhism.

Bud dhism (bü′diz əm, bùd′iz əm), *n.* religion based on the teachings of Buddha which maintains that right living will enable people to attain nirvana, a condition free from all desire and pain.

Bud dhist (bü′dist, bùd′ist), *n.* person who believes in and follows the teachings of Buddha. —*adj.* of Buddha, his followers, or the religion founded by him: *a Buddhist temple.*

Buddha

ca dav er (kə dav′ər), *n.* a dead body; corpse.

can vas (kan′vəs), *n.* **1** a strong cloth with a coarse weave made of cotton, flax, or hemp, used to make tents, sails, certain articles of clothing, etc. **2** something made of or covered with canvas. **3** piece of canvas on which an oil painting is painted. **4** an oil painting.

case ment (kās′mənt), *n.* **1** window or part of a window which opens on hinges like a door. **2** any window.

cir cum vent (sėr′kəm vent′), *v.t.* **1** get the better of or defeat by trickery; outwit: *circumvent the law.* **2** go around.

con firm (kən fėrm′), *v.t.* **1** prove to be true or correct; make certain: *confirm a rumor.* **2** approve by formal consent; approve; consent to: *The Senate confirmed the treaty.* **3** make firmer; strengthen: *A sudden storm confirmed my decision not to leave.* **—con firm′a ble,** *adj.*

con tem po rar y (kən tem′pə rer′ē), *adj., n., pl.* **-rar ies.** *—adj.* **1** belonging to or living in the same period of time: *Walt Whitman and Emily Dickinson were contemporary poets.* **2** of the same age or date: *contemporary trees.* **3** of or having to do with the present time; modern: *contemporary literature.* *—n.* **1** person living in the same period of time as another or others. **2** person or thing of the same age or date.

co ro na tion (kôr′ə nā′shən, kor′ə nā′shən), *n.* ceremony of crowning a king, queen, emperor, etc.

cour i er (kėr′ē ər, kúr′ē ər), *n.* **1** messenger sent in haste: *Government dispatches were sent by couriers.* **2** a secret agent who transfers information to and from other agents.

a hat	oi oil
ā age	ou out
ä far	u cup
e let	ů put
ē equal	ü rule
ėr term	
i it	ch child
ī ice	ng long
o hot	sh she
ō open	th thin
ô order	ᴛʜ then
	zh measure
ə = {	a in about e in taken i in pencil o in lemon u in circus
< = derived from	

Der by (dėr′bē; *British* där′bē), *n., pl.* **-bies.** **1** a famous horse race run every year since 1780 at Epsom Downs. **2** a horse race of similar importance: *the Kentucky Derby.* **3 derby, a** any important race or competition. **b** a stiff hat with a rounded crown and a narrow brim; bowler. **4** city in central England. 216,000. [< the 12th Earl of *Derby,* died 1834, who founded this horse race]

de scend ant (di sen′dənt), *n.* **1** person born of a certain family or group. **2** offspring; child, grandchild, great-grandchild, etc. You are a direct descendant of your parents, grandparents, great-grandparents, and earlier ancestors.

dis sect (di sekt′, dī sekt′), *v.t.* **1** cut apart (an animal, plant, etc.) in order to examine or study the structure. **2** examine carefully part by part; criticize in detail; analyze.

draught (draft), *n., v.t., adj.* draft. **—draught′-er,** *n.*

derby (def. 3b)

dur a ble (dùr/ə bəl, dyùr/ə bəl), *adj.* 1 able to withstand wear, decay, etc.: *durable fabric.* 2 lasting a long time: *a durable peace.* —**dur/a bil/i ty,** *n.* —**dur/a ble ness,** *n.* —**dur/a bly,** *adv.*

Elizabeth I

Elizabeth I, 1533-1603, queen of England from 1558 to 1603, daughter of Henry VIII and Anne Boleyn.

E liz a be than (i liz/ə bē/thən, i liz/ə beth/ən), *adj.* of the time when Elizabeth I ruled England. —*n.* Englishman, especially a writer, of the time of Elizabeth I: *Shakespeare is a famous Elizabethan.*

em pire (em/pīr; *usually* äm pir/ *for adj.*), *n.* 1 group of countries or states under one ruler or government: *The Roman Empire consisted of many separate territories.* 2 country that has an emperor or empress: *the Japanese Empire.* 3 absolute power; supreme authority. 4 a large business or group of businesses under the control of a single person, family, syndicate, etc. —*adj.* **Empire,** of or having to do with a style of dress, furniture, etc., in fashion during the first French empire (1804-1815). characterized by formal and complex design.

fab u lous (fab/yə ləs), *adj.* 1 not believable; amazing: *That antique shop asks fabulous prices.* 2 of or belonging to a fable; imaginary: *The phoenix is a fabulous bird.* 3 like a fable. 4 INFORMAL. wonderful; exciting.

fer tile (fèr/tl), *adj.* 1 able to bear seeds, fruit, young, etc.; capable of reproduction. 2 capable of developing into a new individual; fertilized: *Chicks hatch from fertile eggs.* 3 able to produce much; producing crops easily: *Fertile soil yields good crops.* 4 producing ideas; creative: *a fertile mind.*

gar ri son (gar/ə sən), *n.* 1 group of soldiers stationed in a fort, town, etc., to defend it. 2 place that has a garrison. —*v.t.* 1 station soldiers in (a fort, town, etc.) to defend it. 2 occupy (a fort, town, etc.) as a garrison.

haunch (hônch, hänch), *n.* 1 hip. 2 **haunches,** *pl.* the hindquarters of an animal: *The dog sat on his haunches.* 3 the leg and loin of a deer, sheep, or other animal, used for food.

head dress (hed/dres/), *n.* 1 a covering or decoration for the head. 2 way of wearing or arranging the hair.

hea then (hē′ᵺən), *n., pl.* **-thens** or **-then,** *adj.*
—*n.* **1** person who does not believe in the God of
the Bible; person who is not a Christian, Jew, or
Moslem; pagan. **2** people who are heathens.
3 person without religion or culture; unenlightened person. —*adj.* **1** of or having to do with
heathens; not Christian, Jewish, or Moslem.
2 not religious or cultured; unenlightened.
—**hea′then ness,** *n.*
hos tile (hos′tl; *sometimes* hos′tīl), *adj.* **1** of an
enemy or enemies: *the hostile army.* **2** opposed;
unfriendly; unfavorable. —*n.* a hostile person;
enemy. —**hos′tile ly,** *adv.*

im mor tal (i môr′tl), *adj.* **1** living forever; never
dying; everlasting. **2** of or having to do with
immortal beings or immortality; divine.
3 remembered or famous forever. —*n.* **1** an
immortal being. **2** person remembered or famous forever.
in her ent (in hir′ənt, in her′ənt), *adj.* belonging
to a person or thing as a permanent and essential
quality or attribute; intrinsic: *inherent honesty,
the inherent sweetness of sugar.* —**in her′ent-
ly,** *adv.*

liege (lēj), *n.* in the Middle Ages: **1** lord having a
right to the homage and loyal service of his
vassals. **2** vassal obliged to give homage and
loyal service to his lord; liegeman. —*adj.*
1 having a right to the homage and loyal service
of vassals. **2** obliged to give homage and loyal
service to a lord.

man u mis sion (man′yə mish′ən), *n.* **1** a freeing
from slavery. **2** a being freed from slavery.
mete (mēt), *v.t.,* **met ed, met ing. 1** give to each
person a proper or fair share; distribute; allot:
The judge will mete out praise and blame.
2 ARCHAIC. measure. [Old English *metan*]
mys tic (mis′tik), *adj.* **1** mystical. **2** having to do
with the ancient religious mysteries or other
occult rites: *mystic arts.* **3** of or having to do
with mystics or mysticism. **4** of hidden meaning
or nature; enigmatical; mysterious. —*n.* person
who believes that union with God or knowledge
of truths inaccessible to the ordinary powers of
the mind can be attained through faith, spiritual
insight, intuition, or exaltation of feeling.

o pi um (ō′pē əm), *n.* a powerful narcotic drug
containing morphine and other alkaloids, made
by drying the milky juice from the unripened
capsule of the opium poppy. Opium is valuable
in medicine but it is dangerously habit-forming.

a	hat	oi	oil
ā	age	ou	out
ä	far	u	cup
e	let	ù	put
ē	equal	ü	rule
ėr	term		
i	it	ch	child
ī	ice	ng	long
o	hot	sh	she
ō	open	th	thin
ô	order	ᴛʜ	then
		zh	measure

ə = { a in about / e in taken / i in pencil / o in lemon / u in circus

< = derived from

or tho dox (ôr/thə doks), *adj.* **1** generally accepted, especially in religion. **2** having generally accepted views or opinions, especially in religion; adhering to established customs and traditions: *an orthodox Methodist.* **3 Orthodox,** of or having to do with the Eastern Church or any of various national churches conforming to its doctrines. **4 Orthodox,** of or having to do with the branch of Judaism adhering most closely to ancient ritual, customs, and traditions. **5** approved by convention; usual; customary.

par ox ysm (par/ək siz/əm), *n.* **1** a sudden, severe attack of the symptoms of a disease, usually recurring periodically: *a paroxysm of coughing.* **2** a sudden outburst of emotion or activity: *a paroxysm of rage.*

pau per (pô/pər), *n.* **1** a very poor person. **2** person supported by charity or public welfare.

pie bald (pī/bôld/), *adj.* spotted in two colors, especially black and white: *a piebald horse.* —*n.* a piebald animal, especially a horse.

pig ment (pig/mənt), *n.* **1** a coloring matter, especially a powder or some easily pulverized dry substance that constitutes a paint or dye when mixed with oil, water, or some other liquid. **2** the natural substance occurring in and coloring the tissues of an organism. —*v.t.* color with or as if with pigment.

pike¹ (pīk), *n.* a long wooden shaft with a sharp-pointed metal head; spear. Foot soldiers used to carry pikes.

pike² (pīk), *n.* a sharp point, pointed tip, or spike, such as the head of an arrow or spear.

pike³ (pīk), *n., pl.* **pikes** or **pike. 1** any of a family of large, slender, predatory, freshwater fishes of the Northern Hemisphere, having spiny fins and a long, pointed head, such as the muskellunge and pickerel. **2** any of certain similar fishes, such as the pike perch. [apparently short for *pikefish* <*pike²* + *fish*].

pike⁴ (pīk), *n.* **1** turnpike. **2** **come down the pike,** INFORMAL. appear; show up.

pil grim age (pil/grə mij), *n.* **1** a pilgrim's journey; journey to some sacred place as an act of religious devotion. **2** a long journey.

pin nace (pin/is), *n.* **1** a ship's boat. **2** any light sailing vessel.

pinnace (def.1)

Pur i tan (pyùr/ə tən), *n.* **1** member of a group in the Church of England during the 1500's and 1600's who wanted simpler forms of worship and stricter morals. Many Puritans settled in New England. **2 puritan,** person who is very strict in morals and religion. —*adj.* **1** of the Puritans. **2 puritan,** very strict in morals and religion.

re pulse (ri puls/), v., -pulsed, -puls ing, n. —v.t.
1 drive back; repel. 2 refuse to accept; reject:
She repulsed my invitation. —n. 1 a driving or
a being driven back; repulsion: *After the second
repulse, the enemy surrendered.* 2 refusal; rejec-
tion.

re sign (ri zīn/), v.t. 1 give up (a job, position,
etc.): *resign the presidency.* 2 **resign oneself,**
submit quietly; adapt oneself without complaint;
yield. —v.i. give up a job, position, etc.

ro tar y (rō/tər ē), adj. 1 turning like a top or a
wheel; rotating. 2 (of motion) circular. 3 having
parts that rotate. 4 of or having to do with a
rotary engine. —n. a rotary engine or machine.

sam u rai (sam/ù rī/), n., pl. -rai. 1 the military
class in feudal Japan, consisting of the retainers
of the great nobles. 2 member of this class.

scep ter (sep/tər), n. 1 the rod or staff carried by a
ruler as a symbol of royal power or authority.
2 royal or imperial power or authority; sovereign-
ty. Also, **sceptre.**

skull cap (skul/kap/), n. a close-fitting cap without a brim.

stal lion (stal/yən), n. an uncastrated male horse,
especially one kept for breeding purposes.

steed (stēd), n. 1 horse, especially a riding horse.
2 a high-spirited horse.

stone ma son (stōn/mā/sn), n. person who cuts
stone or builds walls, etc., of stone.

swoon (swün), v.i. 1 faint: *swoon at the sight of
blood.* 2 fade or die away gradually. —n. a faint.

treach er y (trech/ər ē), n., pl. -er ies. 1 a break-
ing of faith; treacherous behavior; deceit.
2 treason.

trough (trôf, trof), n. 1 a narrow, open, boxlike
container for holding food or water, especially
for farm stock or other animals. 2 something
shaped like this: *The baker used a trough for
kneading dough.* 3 a channel for carrying water;
gutter. 4 a long hollow between two ridges,
especially the hollow between two waves or two
hills.

vouch (vouch), v.i. 1 be responsible; give a guaran-
tee (for): *I can vouch for the truth of the story.
The principal vouched for the student's honesty.*
2 give evidence or assurance (for): *The success of
the campaign guarantees for the candidate's popu-
larity.* —v.t. 1 declare; confirm. 2 support or sub-
stantiate (a statement, etc.) to be true or accurate;
title, etc.). 3 cite or appeal to
(authority, example, a passage in a book, etc.) in
support of verification.

a hat	oi oil
ā age	ou out
ä far	u cup
e let	ú put
ē equal	ü rule
ėr term	
i it	ch child
ī ice	ng long
o hot	sh she
ō open	th thin
ô order	ŦH then
	zh measure

ə = { a in about
e in taken
i in pencil
o in lemon
u in circus

< = derived from

Queen Elizabeth II
with **scepter** (def. 1)

ACKNOWLEDGMENTS

Text

Page 8: "What Is This Place?" from *The Princess in the Pigpen* by Jane Resh Thomas. Text copyright © 1989 by Jane Resh Thomas. Reprinted by permission of Clarion Books, a Houghton Mifflin Company imprint.

Page 22: "Creativity Exercises and the Princess" by Jane Resh Thomas. Copyright © 1991 by Jane Resh Thomas.

Page 26: "A Story That Could Be True" by William Stafford. Copyright © 1976 by William Stafford. Reprinted by permission of the author.

Page 27: "Luther and Breck" Text from *Bronzeville Boys and Girls* by Gwendolyn Brooks. Copyright © 1956 by Gwendolyn Brooks Blakely. Reprinted by permission of HarperCollins Publishers.

Page 28: "The Prince and the Pauper" by Mark Twain from *Stage Plays from the Classics* by Joellen Bland. Copyright © 1987 by Joellen Bland. Reprinted by permission of Plays, Inc.

Page 52: "People of the Four Quarters" was condensed from *The Grandchildren of the Incas*, by Ritva Lehtinen with photographs by Matti A. Pitkänen. Original copyright 1984, by the photographer. Published in 1991 by Carolrhoda Books Inc., Minneapolis, MN 55401. Used with permission of the publisher. All rights reserved.

Page 60: "The Gold of West Africa" by Mary Daniels. Copyright © 1991 by Mary Daniels.

Page 64: "Leonardo da Vinci" from *Experimenting with Inventions* by Robert Gardner. Copyright © 1990 by Robert Gardner. Reproduced with permission of the publisher, Franklin Watts, Inc.

Page 72: "Hats to Believe In" by Margaret Cooper. From *Faces* June 1985 issue: *We Wear Many Hats*, © 1985, Cobblestone Publishing, Inc., Peterborough, NY 03458. Reprinted by permission of the publisher.

Page 80: "The Wonder Worker" from *Once Upon a Horse* by Suzanne Jurmain. Copyright © 1989 by Suzanne Jurmain. Published by Lothrop, Lee & Shepard Books. Reprinted by permission of William Morrow & Company, Inc./Publishers, New York.

Page 88: "First Glimpse of America" from *The Witch of Blackbird Pond* by Elizabeth George Speare. Copyright © 1958 by Elizabeth George Speare. Reprinted by permission of Houghton Mifflin Company.

Page 102: "Research Spelled Fun" by Elizabeth George Speare. Copyright © 1991 by Elizabeth George Speare.

Page 106: "Historical Fiction: An Opportunity and Challenge" by Violet Harris. Copyright © 1991 by Violet Harris.

Page 107: First four lines from "Heritage" by Countee Cullen. Reprinted by permission of GRM Associates Inc., Agents of the estate of Ida M. Cullen from the book *On These I Stand* by Countee Cullen. Copyright 1925 by Harper & Brothers; copyright renewed 1953 by Ida M. Cullen.

Page 110: Excerpt from *I, Juan de Pareja*, retitled "I Am Set Free" by Elizabeth Borton de Treviño. Copyright © 1965 by Elizabeth Borton de Treviño. Reprinted by permission of Farrar, Straus and Giroux, Inc.

Page 124: "History" from *The Panther and the Lash* by Langston Hughes. Copyright © 1967 by Arna Bontemps and George Houston Bass. Reprinted by permission of Alfred A. Knopf, Inc.

Page 125: "In the Museum" from *Everything Glistens and Everything Sings*, copyright © 1987 by Charlotte Zolotow, reprinted by permission of Harcourt Brace Jovanovich, Inc.

Page 126: "What a Precious Gift, Life" from *A Samurai's Tale* by Erik Christian Haugaard. Copyright © 1984 by Erik Christian Haugaard. Reprinted by permission of Houghton Mifflin Company.

ARTISTS

Pol Turgeon, Cover, 1, 3, 4–5, 133
Barrett Root, 8, 15, 19, 25
Naomi Spellman, 22, 102
Chris Froeter, 26–27, 55, 124–125
Bill Russell, 28, 36, 43, 50, 51
Greg Drasler, 72, 74–75, 79
Vince Mancuso, 88, 96–97, 105
Graham Baker, 126

PHOTOGRAPHS

Page 6: The Huntington Library and Art Gallery, San Marino, CA
Page 7: NASA
Page 10: from *The Annotated Shakespeare*
Page 11: Martha Swope
Page 17: COMSTOCK INC.
Page 22: Courtesy of Jane Resh Thomas
Page 32: North Wind Picture Archives
Page 33: Milt & Joan Mann/Cameramann International, Ltd.
Page 47: D. MacTavish/COMSTOCK INC.
Page 57: George Hunter/H. Armstrong Roberts
Page 60: Jean Paul Barbier/Musee Barbier-Muller, Geneva
Pages 62, 63: Pierre-Alain Ferrazzini/Musee Barbier-Muller, Geneva
Pages 67, 71: Courtesy of the Trustees of the British Museum
Page 69: Mark Greenberg/Visions
Page 76: North Wind Picture Archives
Page 77: David Needham/Envision
Page 80: J. M. de America, Madrid
Page 85: R. Wall/H. Armstrong Roberts
Page 94: National Maritime Museum, Prinshendrik, The Netherlands
Page 95: Milt & Joan Mann/Cameramann International, Ltd.
Page 102: Courtesy of Elizabeth George Speare
Page 106: Lee Boltin
Page 110: The Metropolitan Museum of Art
Page 115: Madrid, Prado/Art Resource
Page 118: Alinari/Art Resource
Page 120: Apsley House, London/Art Resource
Page 129: NASA
Illustrations owned and copyrighted by the illustrator.

GLOSSARY

The contents of the Glossary entries in this book have been adapted from *Advanced Dictionary*, Copyright © 1988, by Scott, Foresman and Company.
Page 138: Seattle Art Museum/Eugene Fuller Memorial Collection
Page 139: Barbara Frankel
Page 140: Marquess of Salisbury
Page 142: Cathy Koehler
Page 143: Cecil Beaton, London, England